CW00854434

Automating Microsoft Azure with PowerShell

Automate Microsoft Azure tasks using Windows PowerShell to take full control of your Microsoft Azure deployments

John Chapman

Aman Dhally

PACKT enterprise
professional expertise distilled

PUBLISHING
BIRMINGHAM - MUMBAI

Automating Microsoft Azure with PowerShell

Copyright © 2015 Packt Publishing

All rights reserved. No part of this book may be reproduced, stored in a retrieval system, or transmitted in any form or by any means, without the prior written permission of the publisher, except in the case of brief quotations embedded in critical articles or reviews.

Every effort has been made in the preparation of this book to ensure the accuracy of the information presented. However, the information contained in this book is sold without warranty, either express or implied. Neither the authors, nor Packt Publishing, and its dealers and distributors will be held liable for any damages caused or alleged to be caused directly or indirectly by this book.

Packt Publishing has endeavored to provide trademark information about all of the companies and products mentioned in this book by the appropriate use of capitals. However, Packt Publishing cannot guarantee the accuracy of this information.

First published: March 2015

Production reference: 1110315

Published by Packt Publishing Ltd.
Livery Place
35 Livery Street
Birmingham B3 2PB, UK.

ISBN 978-1-78439-887-3

www.packtpub.com

Credits

Authors
John Chapman
Aman Dhally

Reviewers
Brian Denicola
Chrissy LeMaire
Dmitriy Kataskin

Acquisition Editor
Larissa Pinto

Content Development Editor
Shweta Pant

Technical Editor
Shashank Desai

Copy Editor
Relin Hedly

Project Coordinator
Shipra Chawhan

Proofreaders
Simran Bhogal
Stephen Copestake

Indexer
Hemangini Bari

Graphics
Abhinash Sahu

Production Coordinator
Melwyn D'sa

Cover Work
Melwyn D'sa

About the Author

John Chapman is a software engineer in the Phoenix area. Having also worked in the higher education, telecommunications, and enterprise software industries, John's development experience includes .NET, SharePoint, Swift, Objective-C and other languages, markup, and platforms. You can visit his website at `http://www.johnchapman.net/`.

I would like to thank my wife, Simone. Her support and patience have made what I have accomplished in my life possible.

About the Author

Aman Dhally is a PowerShell MVP and founder of New Delhi PowerShell User Group. He has more than 14 years of experience in the IT industry. His main focus is the automation of manual tasks using PowerShell. He came in to contact with PowerShell in 2010. Since then, he has published a wealth of articles, videos, blogs, and PowerShell scripts. He loves teaching PowerShell and speaking at User Group events.

Aman works as a network analyst for Analysys Mason Limited, which he describes as a "cool" company to work for. Here, he works on various IT projects, and his PowerShell skills bring a unique approach to solving IT issues and improving efficiency within the company.

He is fascinated by anything to do with life: philosophy, self-help techniques, and biographies of famous people, which he finds inspiring. In his free time, you will often find him reading a book on any of these subjects. His philosophy can be summed up by his phrase: "You see a mousetrap, I see free cheese and a challenge!"

Acknowledgments

I would like to thank Waheguru Ji (the almighty God). With your blessings, I was able to complete this book. I know you are always with me when I am lost or when I lose hope, and almost give up. You hold my hand and show me the way. I pray to you that you do the same for every person in this world and bring love, peace, and harmony among mankind.

I dedicate this book to my beloved daughter, Manya Kaur, who is just two-and-a-half years old at the time of writing this book. One day, when you grow up, you'll be proud of your father. I want you to make this world a better place by sharing your knowledge with others. I love you and always will until eternity.

I would like to thank each and every member of the Dhally family who supported me throughout the process of writing this book. You all are rockstars of my life. I love you a lot and wouldn't be here without your support. I am thankful to God for such a beautiful and loving family.

Special thanks to Ben Griffiths who introduced me to PowerShell in 2010, which changed my life. I would like to dedicate this book to Ben too. Thanks for always being there for me.

Many thanks to my lovely friends who always encouraged me and believed in me. I would like to thank all my colleagues at the ICT department for their help and support. Special thanks to my bosses, Rohan Dhamija and David Creighton, who taught me some of the most valuable lessons of life.

I am really thankful to Larissa and Shweta from Packt Publishing. They are like angels, always supporting, encouraging, and inspiring; without their support, this book wouldn't have been published. I would also like to thank all the reviewers, Brian Denicola, Chrissy LeMaire, and Dmitriy Kataskin for their support and help.

Finally, a big thanks to the readers for purchasing this book. I hope you like it.

Keep dreaming, guys; they do come true: "A! Murky Ana".

This book is dedicated to my beloved daughter, Manya Kaur.
–Aman Dhally

About the Reviewers

Brian Denicola is an operations and database manager at a large professional services firm. He has over 15 years of experience in IT and has been scripting PowerShell since Version 1 was released way back in 2006. He has also been using Microsoft Azure on and off since 2008, but his main background is in SharePoint, which is how he stumbled on PowerShell. When he is automating deployments, he loves to spend time with his wonderful wife, Nelie, and three boys, Xander, Gabriel, and Philip. His Twitter handle is `@brianjdenicola` and his blog is `http://quickanddirtyscripting.wordpress.com`.

Chrissy LeMaire has worked in IT for nearly 20 years, and she currently serves as the SQL Server DBA for NATO Special Ops in Belgium. Always an avid scripter, she attended the Monad session at Microsoft's Professional Developers Conference in Los Angeles back in 2005 and has worked and played with PowerShell ever since.

Chrissy is currently pursuing an MS in Systems Engineering at Regis University. In her spare time, she tweets (`@cl`) and maintains two websites, `https://blog.netnerds.net/` and `http://www.realcajunrecipes.com/`.

She also served as a technical reviewer for *Windows PowerShell Cookbook, Lee Holmes, O'Reilly Media.*

www.PacktPub.com

Support files, eBooks, discount offers, and more

For support files and downloads related to your book, please visit www.PacktPub.com.

Did you know that Packt offers eBook versions of every book published, with PDF and ePub files available? You can upgrade to the eBook version at www.PacktPub.com and as a print book customer, you are entitled to a discount on the eBook copy. Get in touch with us at service@packtpub.com for more details.

At www.PacktPub.com, you can also read a collection of free technical articles, sign up for a range of free newsletters and receive exclusive discounts and offers on Packt books and eBooks.

https://www2.packtpub.com/books/subscription/packtlib

Do you need instant solutions to your IT questions? PacktLib is Packt's online digital book library. Here, you can search, access, and read Packt's entire library of books.

Why subscribe?
- Fully searchable across every book published by Packt
- Copy and paste, print, and bookmark content
- On demand and accessible via a web browser

Free access for Packt account holders

If you have an account with Packt at www.PacktPub.com, you can use this to access PacktLib today and view 9 entirely free books. Simply use your login credentials for immediate access.

Instant updates on new Packt books

Get notified! Find out when new books are published by following @PacktEnterprise on Twitter or the *Packt Enterprise* Facebook page.

Table of Contents

Preface

Microsoft Azure offers a plethora of cloud-based services that can integrate into an enterprise organization's data center infrastructures. From Active Directory to virtual machines, organizations that make full use of Azure services have a lot to configure and manage. Using PowerShell, most Azure configuration and management tasks can be streamlined and automated. This book explores using Microsoft Azure PowerShell to manage the commonly used services of Microsoft Azure.

What this book covers

Chapter 1, Getting Started with Azure and PowerShell, introduces Windows PowerShell, configures Microsoft Azure PowerShell tools, and connects to Microsoft Azure using PowerShell.

Chapter 2, Managing Azure Storage with PowerShell, explores managing the services offered by a Microsoft Azure storage account with PowerShell, including file, blob, table, and queue storage.

Chapter 3, Managing Azure Virtual Machines with PowerShell, covers how to create and manage virtual machines in Microsoft Azure using PowerShell.

Chapter 4, Managing Azure SQL Databases with PowerShell, examines the basics of creating and managing SQL databases in Microsoft Azure using PowerShell.

Chapter 5, Deploying and Managing Azure Websites with PowerShell, delves into creating and publishing Microsoft Azure websites with PowerShell.

Chapter 6, Managing Azure Virtual Networks with PowerShell, explores Microsoft Azure virtual networks and how to create and manage them with PowerShell.

Chapter 7, Managing Azure Traffic Manager with PowerShell, investigates how to manage geo-redundant and high-availability services in Microsoft Azure using Microsoft Azure's Traffic Manager with PowerShell.

Chapter 8, Managing Azure Cloud Services with PowerShell, covers how to manage Microsoft Azure cloud services using PowerShell.

Chapter 9, Managing Azure Active Directory with PowerShell, explores how to use and manage Active Directory in Microsoft Azure using PowerShell.

Chapter 10, Automating Azure with PowerShell, covers how to use runbooks to automate Microsoft Azure management tasks using PowerShell.

What you need for this book

Microsoft Azure PowerShell requires Microsoft Windows PowerShell 3.0 or a newer version running on Microsoft Windows 7/Microsoft Windows Server 2008 R2 or newer. Downloading Microsoft Azure PowerShell and related tools is covered in *Chapter 1, Getting Started with Azure and PowerShell*.

Who this book is for

This book is designed for administrators and developers who manage Microsoft Azure services. Administrators will take away knowledge and ideas to better manage and automate tasks for data center operations. Developers will take away knowledge and ideas to better automate tasks for deployments and other application configurations.

 Microsoft Azure provides a platform for developers to build enterprise-level, geo-globally-distributed, and highly-scalable applications. While this book will be useful for developers, it does not delve into building applications and processes on Microsoft Azure.

Conventions

In this book, you will find a number of styles of text that distinguish between different kinds of information. Here are some examples of these styles, and an explanation of their meaning.

Code words in text, database table names, folder names, filenames, file extensions, pathnames, dummy URLs, user input, and Twitter handles are shown as follows: "Many of the cmdlets used to instantiate new services, such as a website, in Microsoft Azure include a -Location parameter."

A block of code is set as follows:

```
<?xml version="1.0" encoding="utf-8"?>
<NetworkConfiguration
xmlns="http://schemas.microsoft.com/ServiceHosting/2011/07/Network
Configuration">
  <VirtualNetworkConfiguration>
    <Dns>
      <DnsServers>
        <DnsServer name="DNS1" IPAddress="10.10.1.1"/>
      </DnsServers>
    </Dns>
```

Any command-line input or output is written as follows:

```
PS C:\> New-AzureSqlDatabaseServerFirewallRule -RuleName
"MyIPAddress" -ServerName "jztfvtq0e1" -StartIpAddress
123.123.123.123 -EndIpAddress 123.123.123.123
```

New terms and **important words** are shown in bold. Words that you see on the screen, in menus or dialog boxes for example, appear in the text like this: "Navigate to the left-hand side of the page and select **Websites**".

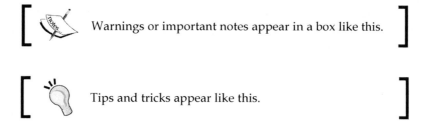

Warnings or important notes appear in a box like this.

Tips and tricks appear like this.

Reader feedback

Feedback from our readers is always welcome. Let us know what you think about this book—what you liked or may have disliked. Reader feedback is important for us to develop titles that you really get the most out of.

To send us general feedback, simply send an e-mail to feedback@packtpub.com, and mention the book title via the subject of your message.

If there is a topic that you have expertise in and you are interested in either writing or contributing to a book, see our author guide on www.packtpub.com/authors.

Customer support

Now that you are the proud owner of a Packt book, we have a number of things to help you to get the most from your purchase.

Downloading the example code

You can download the example code files for all Packt books you have purchased from your account at http://www.packtpub.com. If you purchased this book elsewhere, you can visit http://www.packtpub.com/support and register to have the files e-mailed directly to you.

Errata

Although we have taken every care to ensure the accuracy of our content, mistakes do happen. If you find a mistake in one of our books—maybe a mistake in the text or the code—we would be grateful if you could report this to us. By doing so, you can save other readers from frustration and help us improve subsequent versions of this book. If you find any errata, please report them by visiting http://www.packtpub.com/submit-errata, selecting your book, clicking on the **Errata Submission Form** link, and entering the details of your errata. Once your errata are verified, your submission will be accepted and the errata will be uploaded to our website or added to any list of existing errata under the Errata section of that title.

To view the previously submitted errata, go to https://www.packtpub.com/books/content/support and enter the name of the book in the search field. The required information will appear under the **Errata** section.

Piracy

Piracy of copyright material on the Internet is an ongoing problem across all media. At Packt, we take the protection of our copyright and licenses very seriously. If you come across any illegal copies of our works, in any form, on the Internet, please provide us with the location address or website name immediately so that we can pursue a remedy.

Please contact us at copyright@packtpub.com with a link to the suspected pirated material.

We appreciate your help in protecting our authors, and our ability to bring you valuable content.

Questions

You can contact us at questions@packtpub.com if you are having a problem with any aspect of the book, and we will do our best to address it.

1
Getting Started with Azure and PowerShell

Microsoft Azure (formerly Windows Azure) is a cloud computing service provided by Microsoft. Azure provides the platform and infrastructure to deploy and manage applications and services through a global network of datacenters. These services include websites, databases, virtual machines, message queuing, identity management, content delivery, and so on.

Microsoft is continually adding new services and features to services provided in Microsoft Azure. To keep yourself updated on the latest Azure offerings, subscribe to the Microsoft Azure blog at `http://azure.microsoft.com/blog/`. In addition, the Microsoft Azure website provides detailed information on all current Azure offerings at `http://azure.microsoft.com`.

With Microsoft Azure geared to supplement and integrate into the infrastructure of large enterprise organizations, many organizations apply their data center operation policies and methodologies to their Azure implementations. For many of these organizations, scripting deployment, configuration, and management tasks is a must.

Much like other Microsoft server products (Exchange Server and SharePoint Server for example), Microsoft Azure services and products can be instantiated, configured, and managed using Windows PowerShell. Using PowerShell, we can automate and script many of the deployment, configuration, and management tasks that are common to data center operations.

From connecting to Microsoft Azure to managing Active Directory instances on Azure, this book will cover how to automate and script common tasks to manage Microsoft Azure. In this chapter, we will get acquainted with Windows PowerShell and get connected to Microsoft Azure. Lastly, we will create an Azure website to introduce how we can manage Microsoft Azure using Windows PowerShell.

Introducing Windows PowerShell

Windows PowerShell is an automation and configuration framework provided by Microsoft. It comprises a command-line shell and a scripting language built on the Microsoft .NET Framework. The commands used in PowerShell are referred to as **cmdlets** and, typically, have a verb prefix followed by a topical command name. For instance, the cmdlet to add a computer to an Active Directory domain is Add-Computer.

> Nearly all Microsoft-provided cmdlets for PowerShell include help content that can be accessed using the Get-Help cmdlet. To retrieve help content for the Add-Computer cmdlet, for instance, you would simply enter Get-Help Add-Computer.

Modules and snap-ins that have been imported into the current PowerShell session provide the cmdlets in PowerShell. The core modules bundled with PowerShell provide the cmdlets that are available out of the box with PowerShell. Other Microsoft server products, such as Microsoft SharePoint Server (the 2010 version and higher) and Microsoft Exchange Server (the 2007 version and higher), provide modules and snap-ins that make cmdlets specific to these products available in a PowerShell session.

The following screenshot shows what the PowerShell Command Prompt looks like. The default color scheme for PowerShell windows is gray text on a dark blue background; for clarity, however, when printed or viewed in black and white, the screenshots used in this book use black text on a white background.

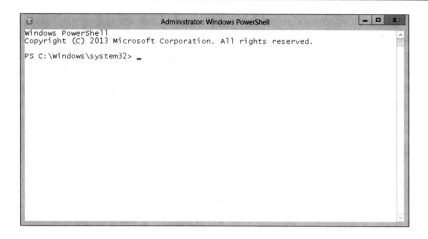

With PowerShell built on the Microsoft .NET Framework, .NET classes and methods can be used directly from the Command Prompt. For instance, while the `Get-Date` cmdlet will return a `System.DateTime` object, we can also accomplish the same task by entering `[System.DateTime]::Now`, as shown in the following screenshot. This is particularly useful when creating complex scripts that require using .NET classes and methods not already exposed as cmdlets.

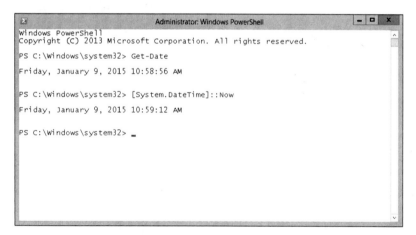

When accessing a static method or property of a .NET class, the full class name (with its namespace) is placed in square brackets (`[` and `]`). The method name or property name is then placed after two semicolons (`::`). For instance, accessing the `Now` property of `System.DateTime` is written as `[System.DateTime]::Now`, and accessing the `IsLeapYear` method of `System.DateTime` is written as `[System.DateTime]::IsLeapYear(2020)`. It's not required to know how to interact directly with .NET classes and methods when using PowerShell. However, this is useful when functionality needs to be extended beyond what the available cmdlets can do.

In addition to the Windows PowerShell Command Prompt, Microsoft has provided the Windows PowerShell **Integrated Scripting Environment** (**ISE**). PowerShell ISE is an application specifically designed to write PowerShell scripts. It includes IntelliSense, the Command Prompt, and a list of available cmdlets. The examples throughout this book will use the PowerShell Command Prompt, as shown in the preceding screenshot. However, you can use the PowerShell ISE to complete any of the examples provided:

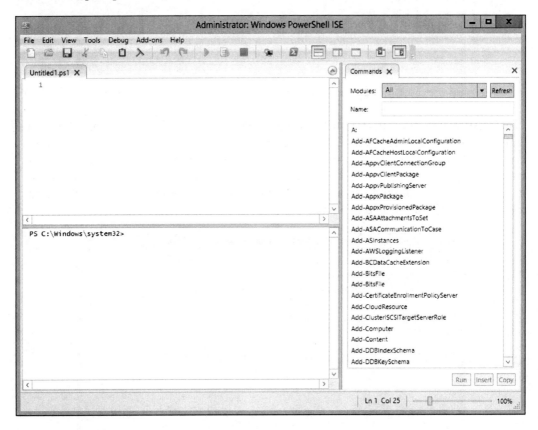

Windows PowerShell is included in Windows, starting with Windows 7 and Windows Server 2008 R2. The following table indicates which version of PowerShell is included with each version of Windows:

PowerShell version	Windows versions
PowerShell 2.0	Windows 7, Windows Server 2008 R2
PowerShell 3.0	Windows 8, Windows Server 2012
PowerShell 4.0	Windows 8.1, Windows Server 2012 R2

Using PowerShell to manage Microsoft Azure requires PowerShell 3.0 or higher. Windows 7 and Windows Server 2008 R2 do not include a supported version of PowerShell. In order to manage Microsoft Azure on Windows 7 or Windows Server 2008 R2, the Windows Management Framework will need to be updated to version 3.0 or higher. To download the Windows Management Framework 3.0 (which includes PowerShell 3.0), visit `http://www.microsoft.com/en-us/download/details.aspx?id=34595`, and to download the Windows Management Framework 4.0 (which includes PowerShell 4.0), visit `http://www.microsoft.com/en-us/download/details.aspx?id=40855`.

While PowerShell 4.0 and higher are not required to manage Microsoft Azure, each subsequent version of PowerShell after 3.0 has enhanced the overall capabilities of the framework. To upgrade to a newer version of PowerShell, download the latest version of the Windows Management Framework.

For more information about Windows PowerShell and Microsoft Azure, see the following resources:

- Scripting with Windows PowerShell (`http://technet.microsoft.com/en-us/library/bb978526.aspx`)
- Windows PowerShell (`http://en.wikipedia.org/wiki/Windows_PowerShell`)
- Microsoft Azure website (`http://azure.microsoft.com`)
- Windows Management Framework 3.0 download (`http://www.microsoft.com/en-us/download/details.aspx?id=34595`)
- Windows Management Framework 4.0 download (`http://www.microsoft.com/en-us/download/details.aspx?id=40855`)

Connecting to Microsoft Azure using PowerShell

Before using PowerShell cmdlets for Microsoft Azure, we must first have an active Microsoft Azure subscription, install the necessary prerequisites, and connect to the Microsoft Azure subscription. In addition, as Microsoft Azure is a cloud service, we must have an Internet connection in order to manage it.

Microsoft Azure subscriptions

Microsoft Azure is a subscription-based service, typically billed monthly. **Microsoft Developer Network (MSDN)** subscribers receive a free monthly credit for development purposes. In addition, Microsoft offers a free trial of Microsoft Azure for one month (up to $200 worth of services). To sign up for the free trial, visit http://azure.microsoft.com/en-us/pricing/free-trial.

For the purposes of the examples provided in this book, it does not matter what type of Microsoft Azure subscription is used. It simply must be active and you need global administrator rights to the subscription.

 If someone else manages the Microsoft Azure subscription you are using, they can grant you the appropriate access by logging in to the Azure portal and navigating to the settings section of the portal.

Software prerequisites

To manage Microsoft Azure with Windows PowerShell requires the following prerequisites:

- Windows client operating system (Windows 7 or newer) or Windows server operating system (Windows Server 2008 R2 or newer)
- Windows PowerShell 3.0 or newer (bundled with the Windows Management Framework)
- Microsoft Azure PowerShell

While managing the operating system is outside the scope of this book, it is a good idea to ensure that the Windows operating system is up-to-date with the latest security updates and service packs.

Windows PowerShell 3.0 or newer

The Microsoft Azure PowerShell management tools require at least PowerShell 3.0. If the computer is running Windows 8 (or newer) or Windows Server 2012 (or newer), no additional configuration is required for PowerShell. Since Windows 7 and Windows Server 2008 R2 are bundled with PowerShell 2.0, an updated version of the Windows Management Framework will need to be installed.

If the computer is running Windows 7 or Windows Server 2008 R2, follow these steps to verify that PowerShell 3.0 or newer is installed:

1. Open Windows PowerShell from the Start menu.

2. Enter $PSVersionTable in Command Prompt and press *Enter*. The PSVersion property will display the installed version of PowerShell, as shown here:

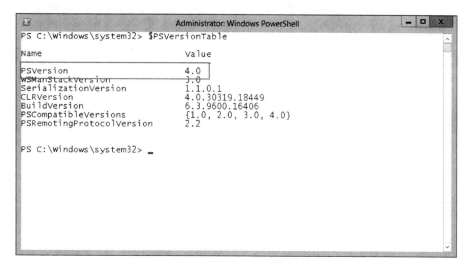

3. If the PowerShell version, as mentioned in step 2, is not 3.0 or greater, download and install a newer version of the Windows Management Framework. To download the Windows Management Framework 3.0 (which includes PowerShell 3.0), visit http://www.microsoft.com/en-us/download/details.aspx?id=34595. To download the Windows Management Framework 4.0 (which includes PowerShell 4.0), visit http://www.microsoft.com/en-us/download/details.aspx?id=40855.

Microsoft Azure PowerShell

Microsoft Azure PowerShell installs a PowerShell module that provides the cmdlets used to manage Microsoft Azure.

> The Microsoft Azure PowerShell project is open source. If desired, you can download the source code for the project and use it, rather than using the official version. The project is hosted on GitHub at https://github.com/Azure/azure-powershell. In addition, each version of Microsoft Azure PowerShell can be obtained from https://github.com/Azure/azure-sdk-tools/releases.

To install Microsoft Azure PowerShell, we will use the following steps:

1. Install the Microsoft Web Platform Installer from `http://www.microsoft.com/web/downloads/platform.aspx`.

2. Open the Microsoft Web Platform Installer.

3. Search for `Microsoft Azure PowerShell`.

4. Select **Add** for **Microsoft Azure PowerShell (Standalone)**, as shown in the following screenshot:

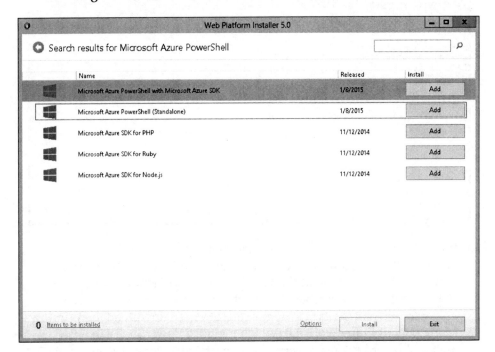

 Developers can select **Microsoft Azure PowerShell with Microsoft Azure SDK** instead to install the development components for Azure in addition to the PowerShell module.

5. Then click on **Install**.

6. Select **I Accept** to accept the Microsoft license terms.

7. Select **Finish**.

8. Finally, close the Web Platform Installer.

Connecting to a Microsoft Azure subscription

Prior to running cmdlets to manage Microsoft Azure, we need to connect to a Microsoft Azure subscription. There are three ways to connect to an Azure subscription:

- Using Azure Active Directory credentials
- Using a publish settings file
- Using an uploaded management certificate

The third option, using an uploaded management certificate, requires developer tools to be installed on the local machine. This is outside the scope of this book. If you would like more information on using a management certificate with Microsoft Azure, refer to http://msdn.microsoft.com/en-us/library/azure/gg551722.aspx.

Connecting to Azure using Azure Active Directory credentials

Connecting to Azure subscription using Azure Active Directory credential is a fairly simple process. One drawback, however, is that you need to enter your credentials each time you start a new Azure PowerShell session, or every 12 hours if the session is kept open.

To automate data center operations, entering credentials for each session might not be ideal. Therefore, consider using a publish settings file, as outlined in the next section, *Connecting to Azure using a publish settings file*, or consider using a management certificate (http://msdn.microsoft.com/en-us/library/azure/gg551722.aspx).

Use the following steps to connect to Microsoft Azure using Azure Active Directory credentials:

1. Open Microsoft Azure PowerShell from the Start menu.

If you are having trouble finding the link in the Start menu, use the search box in the Start menu.

2. Use the `Add-AzureAccount` cmdlet by entering it in the Command Prompt and pressing *Enter*, as shown here:

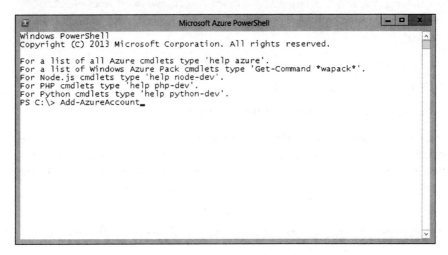

3. When prompted, enter the e-mail address for the account used to manage Microsoft Azure and select **Continue** (the Microsoft account, using your e-mail address, used when creating an Azure subscription is automatically added to an instance of Azure Active Directory):

4. Enter the password for your account and select **Sign in**.

5. Once the sign-in is complete, the Command Prompt will indicate that the account has been added and will indicate which subscription has been selected, as shown here:

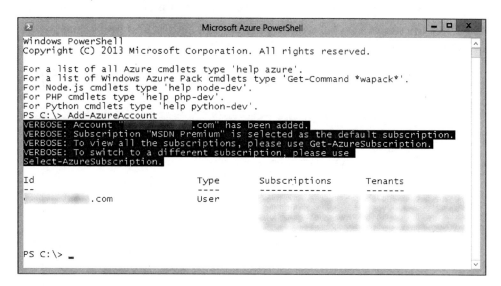

 If you have multiple Microsoft Azure subscriptions that you manage with the same Microsoft account, you can use the `Select-AzureSubscription` cmdlet to switch between subscriptions in the PowerShell session.

Connecting to Azure using a publish settings file

For many automated data center operations, manually entering user credentials for each PowerShell session (or every 12 hours) can be cumbersome. Alternatively, a publish settings file can be downloaded from Azure that allows PowerShell sessions to connect without entering user credentials. This is useful for highly automated processes that do not have human interaction (such as a scheduled backup job).

To connect to Azure using a publish settings file, we will use the following steps to retrieve and import an Azure publish settings file:

1. Open Microsoft Azure PowerShell from the Start menu.

2. Enter the `Get-AzurePublishSettingsFile` cmdlet and press *Enter*, as shown here:

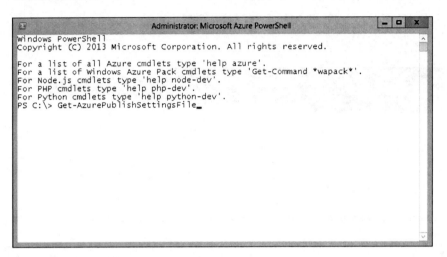

3. The Microsoft Azure portal will be opened in Internet Explorer. If prompted, enter your credentials to log in to the Azure portal.

4. If you have multiple subscriptions associated with your account, you will be prompted to select a subscription, as shown in the following screenshot:

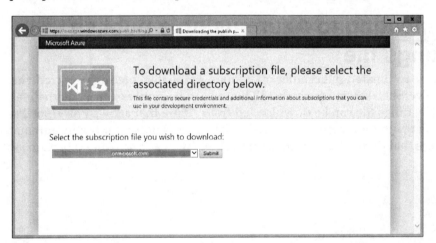

5. When prompted to download the Azure publish settings file, save it to the local computer:

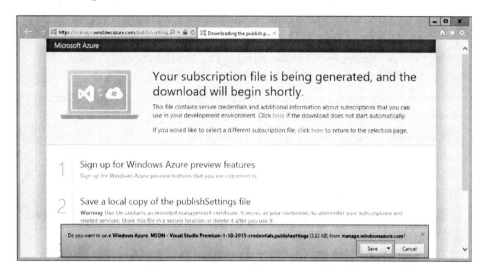

6. In the PowerShell window, use the `Import-AzurePublishSettingsFile` cmdlet (as shown below) to import the Azure publish settings file, which was downloaded in the previous step (`PS C:\> Import-AzurePublishSettingsFile C:\Files\Azure.publishsettings`):

Whether we used the Azure Active Directory credentials method or Azure's publish settings file method, we are now connected to Microsoft Azure in our PowerShell session.

For more information on how to connect to Microsoft Azure with PowerShell and the cmdlets used in this section, refer to the following resources:

- Create and upload a Management Certificate for Azure (`http://msdn.microsoft.com/en-us/library/azure/gg551722.aspx`)

- The `Import-AzurePublishSettingsFile` cmdlet (`http://msdn.microsoft.com/en-us/library/dn495124.aspx`)

- The `Get-AzurePublishSettingsFile` cmdlet (`http://msdn.microsoft.com/en-us/library/dn495224.aspx`)

- The `Select-AzureSubscription` cmdlet (`http://msdn.microsoft.com/en-us/library/dn495203.aspx`)

- The `Add-AzureAccount` cmdlet (`http://msdn.microsoft.com/en-us/library/dn722528.aspx`)

- Microsoft Azure PowerShell Project on GitHub (`https://github.com/Azure/azure-powershell`)

- Microsoft Web Platform Installer download (`http://www.microsoft.com/web/downloads/platform.aspx`)

- Windows Management Framework 3.0 download (`http://www.microsoft.com/en-us/download/details.aspx?id=34595`)

- Windows Management Framework 4.0 download (`http://www.microsoft.com/en-us/download/details.aspx?id=40855`)

Creating a Microsoft Azure website using PowerShell

Now that we are connected to our Microsoft Azure subscription in PowerShell, we will create a simple Azure website to illustrate what we can do with Azure PowerShell.

Many of the cmdlets used to instantiate new services, such as a website, in Microsoft Azure include a `-Location` parameter. This parameter specifies in which Azure data center the new service will be instantiated. To get a list of the data centers available to your subscription, use the `Get-AzureLocation | Format-List -Property Name` command in PowerShell.

To create an Azure website, we will use the following steps:

1. Use the `New-AzureWebsite` cmdlet to create the new Azure website
    (`PS C:\> New-AzureWebsite -Name "PowerShellAutomationIsAwesome"`
    `-Location "WestUS"`). The name specified will be used as part of the
    default hostname of the website and must be unique, as shown in the
    following screenshot:

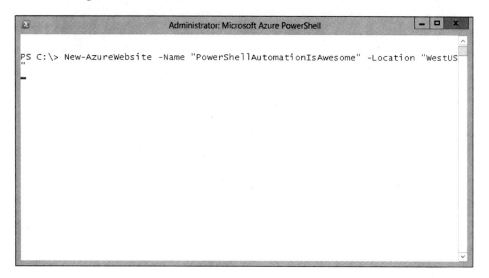

2. When complete, detailed information about the new website will be
    displayed as an output in the Command Prompt window:

3. By default, the URL to the newly created website will be the name used in step 1 with `.azurewebsites.net` appended to it. In this example, the new URL is `http://powershellautomationisawesome.azurewebsites.net`. Navigate to the newly created website in a web browser to observe the results, as shown here:

For more information about the cmdlets used in this section, refer to the following resources:

- The `New-AzureWebsite` cmdlet (`http://msdn.microsoft.com/en-us/library/azure/dn495157.aspx`)

- The `Get-AzureLocation` cmdlet (`http://msdn.microsoft.com/en-us/library/azure/dn495177.aspx`)

Summary

In this chapter, we became acquainted with Windows PowerShell. You learned how to connect Windows PowerShell to Microsoft Azure subscriptions. We will cover many advanced topics related to PowerShell in the course of this book; however, as we cover Azure-specific tasks; however, we will not dig into PowerShell itself (beyond the introduction in this chapter). If you are not yet familiar with using Windows PowerShell, refer to the Scripting with Windows PowerShell article on TechNet at `http://technet.microsoft.com/en-us/library/bb978526.aspx` to get better acquainted with the basic techniques and methodologies of scripting with PowerShell.

In the next chapter, we will explore using PowerShell to manage Azure storage accounts, including file, blob, table, and queue storage.

2
Managing Azure Storage with PowerShell

Microsoft Azure offers a variety of different services to store and retrieve data in the cloud. This includes file, blob, table, and queue storage. Within Azure, each of these types of data is contained within an Azure storage account. While Azure SQL databases are also storage mechanisms, they are not part of an Azure storage account. We will cover Azure SQL databases separately in *Chapter 4, Managing Azure SQL Databases with PowerShell*.

Each of the example tasks covered in this chapter can be accomplished using the latest version of Microsoft Azure PowerShell. However, some tasks, such as file storage, are in preview and not available in the existing Azure management portal found at `https://manage.windowsazure.com`. These are available in the Azure preview portal found at `https://portal.azure.com`. In future, the Azure preview portal will replace the existing Azure management portal.

In this chapter, we will cover the basics of managing Azure storage accounts, including uploading files and blobs, storing data in tables, and managing message queues. In addition, we will apply these concepts by creating a PowerShell script that backs up a folder to Azure blob storage, stores a list of the files in an Azure table, and sends a message to an Azure queue indicating that the operation is completed.

Creating a Microsoft Azure storage account

Before we can upload files or blogs, create tables, or create a queue, we first need a Microsoft Azure storage account.

 To list the storage accounts already associated with the current Azure subscription, use the Get-AzureStorageAccount cmdlet without any parameters.

To create a new Microsoft Azure storage account, we will use the following steps:

1. Open Microsoft Azure PowerShell from the Start menu and connect it to an Azure subscription.

 We must first be connected to Azure in order to create an Azure Storage Account. If not connected to Azure, refer to the *Connecting to a Microsoft Azure subscription* section in *Chapter 1, Getting Started with Azure and PowerShell*.

2. Use the New-AzureStorageAccount cmdlet to create the new storage account (PS C:\> New-AzureStorageAccount -StorageAccountName "psautomation" -Location "West US" -Label "PSAutomation" -Description "Storage account for PSAutomation"). Note that the storage account name provided can only contain numbers and lowercase letters. If any special characters, spaces, or uppercase letters are used, an exception will be thrown:

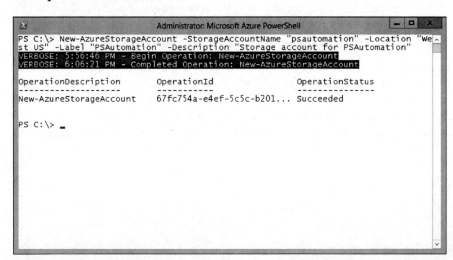

With the new Microsoft Azure storage account created, new default endpoints are also created for each service offered by the storage account:

- Blob service (`http://<StorageAccountName>.blob.core.windows.net`)
- Table service (`http://<StorageAccountName>.table.core.windows.net`)
- Queue service (`http://<StorageAccountName>.queue.core.windows.net`)
- File service (`http://<StorageAccountName>.file.core.windows.net`)

> As Microsoft Azure is a subscription-based service, most instances of a service in Azure will incur cost over time. When a service is no longer being used, deleting the instance will prevent further charges for that item. To delete an Azure storage account that is no longer needed, use the `Remove-AzureStorageAccount` cmdlet with the name of the storage account as the first parameter.

For more information about Microsoft Azure storage accounts and the cmdlet used in this section, see the following resources:

- About Azure Storage accounts (`http://azure.microsoft.com/en-us/documentation/articles/storage-create-storage-account/`)
- The `Remove-AzureStorageAccount` cmdlet (`http://msdn.microsoft.com/en-us/library/azure/dn495212.aspx`)
- The `Get-AzureStorageAccount` cmdlet (`http://msdn.microsoft.com/en-us/library/azure/dn495134.aspx`)
- The `New-AzureStorageAccount` cmdlet (`http://msdn.microsoft.com/en-us/library/azure/dn495115.aspx`)

Azure File storage versus Azure Blob storage

In a Microsoft Azure storage account, both the Azure File storage service and the Azure Blob storage service can be used to store files. Deciding which service to use depends on the purpose of the content and who will use the content. To break down the differences and similarities between these two services, we will cover the features, structure, and common uses for each service.

Azure File storage

Azure File storage provides shared storage using the **Server Message Block (SMB)** protocol. This allows clients, such as Windows Explorer, to connect and browse File storage (such as a typical network file share). In a Windows file share, clients can add directory structures and files to the share. Similar to file shares, Azure File storage is typically used within an organization and not with users outside it.

 Azure File shares can only be mounted in Windows Explorer as a drive within virtual machines running in Azure. They cannot be mounted from computers outside Azure.

A few common uses of Azure File storage include:

- Sharing files between on-premise computers and Azure virtual machines
- Storing application configuration and diagnostic files in a shared location
- Sharing documents and other files with users in the same organization but in different geographical locations

Azure Blob storage

A blob refers to a binary large object, which might not be an actual file. The Azure Blob storage service is used to store large amounts of unstructured data. This data can be accessed via HTTP or HTTPS, making it particularly useful for sharing large amounts of data publicly. Within an Azure storage account, blobs are stored within containers. Each container can be public or private, but it does not offer any directory structure as the File storage service does.

A few common uses of Azure Blob storage include:

- Serving images, style sheets (CSS), and static web files for a website, much like a content delivery network
- Streaming media
- Backups and disaster recovery
- Sharing files to external users

For more information about Microsoft Azure File storage and Azure Blob storage, refer to the following resources:

- How to use Azure File storage (http://azure.microsoft.com/en-us/documentation/articles/storage-dotnet-how-to-use-files/)

- How to use Blob storage from .NET (http://azure.microsoft.com/en-us/documentation/articles/storage-dotnet-how-to-use-blobs/)

Getting the Azure storage account keys

Managing services provided by Microsoft Azure storage accounts requires two pieces of information: the storage account name and an access key. While we can obtain this information from the Microsoft Azure web portal, we will do so with PowerShell.

> Azure storage accounts have a primary and a secondary access key. If one of the access keys is compromised, it can be regenerated without affecting the other.

To obtain the Azure storage account keys, we will use the following steps:

1. Open Microsoft Azure PowerShell from the Start menu and connect it to an Azure subscription.

> We must first be connected to Azure. If not connected to Azure, refer to the *Connecting to a Microsoft Azure subscription* section in *Chapter 1, Getting Started with Azure and PowerShell*.

2. Use the Get-AzureStorageKey cmdlet with the name of the storage account to retrieve the storage account key information and assign it to a variable:

```
PS C:\> $accountKey = Get-AzureStorageKey -
StorageAccountName psautomation
```

3. Use the `Format-List` cmdlet (`PS C:\> $accountKey | Format-List -Property Primary,Secondary`) to display the `Primary` and `Secondary` access key properties. Note that we are using the PowerShell pipeline to use the `Format-List` cmdlet on the `$accountKey` variable:

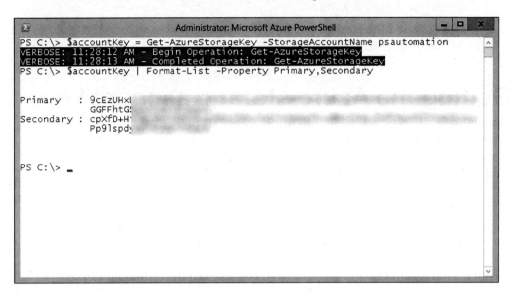

```
Administrator: Microsoft Azure PowerShell                        _ □ X

PS C:\> $accountKey = Get-AzureStorageKey -StorageAccountName psautomation
VERBOSE: 11:28:12 AM - Begin Operation: Get-AzureStorageKey
VERBOSE: 11:28:13 AM - Completed Operation: Get-AzureStorageKey
PS C:\> $accountKey | Format-List -Property Primary,Secondary


Primary    : 9cEzUHxl
             GGFFhtGS
Secondary  : cpXfD+H
             Pp91spd)


PS C:\>
```

4. Assign one of the keys (`Primary` or `Secondary`) to a variable for us to use throughout this chapter:

```
PS C:\> $key = $accountKey.Primary
```

For more information about the PowerShell techniques and cmdlets used in this section, refer to the following resources:

- The `Get-AzureStorageKey` cmdlet (http://msdn.microsoft.com/en-us/library/azure/dn495235.aspx)

- Using the `Format-List` cmdlet (http://technet.microsoft.com/en-us/library/ee176830.aspx)

- Understanding the Windows PowerShell Pipeline (http://technet.microsoft.com/en-us/library/dd347728.aspx)

Using Azure File storage

As mentioned in the *Azure File storage versus Azure Blob storage* section, Azure File services act much like typical network files shares. To demonstrate Azure File services, we will first create a file share. After this, we will create a directory, upload a file, and list the files in a directory.

> Azure File storage is a preview feature for Microsoft Azure at the time of writing this book. It might need to be enabled on your Microsoft Azure subscription before you can use it. Visit `https://account.windowsazure.com/PreviewFeatures` to add the Azure File storage service and any other preview features you wish to test to your subscription.

To complete Azure File storage tasks, we will use the following steps:

1. In the PowerShell session from the *Getting the Azure storage account keys* section in which we obtained an access key, use the `New-AzureStorageContext` cmdlet to connect to the Azure storage account and assign it to a variable. Note that the first parameter is the name of the storage account, whereas the second parameter is the access key:

   ```
   PS C:\> $context = New-AzureStorageContext psautomation $key
   ```

2. Create a new file share using the `New-AzureStorageShare` cmdlet and assign it to a variable:

   ```
   PS C:\> $share = New-AzureStorageShare psautomationshare -Context
   $context
   ```

3. Create a new directory in the file share using the `New-AzureStorageDirectory` cmdlet:

   ```
   PS C:\> New-AzureStorageDirectory -Share $share -Path TextFiles
   ```

4. Before uploading a file to the newly created directory, we need to ensure that we have a file to upload. To create a sample file, we can use the `Set-Content` cmdlet to create a new text file:

   ```
   PS C:\> Set-Content C:\Files\MyFile.txt -Value "Hello"
   ```

5. Upload a file to the newly created directory using the `Set-AzureStorageFileContent` cmdlet:

   ```
   PS C:\> Set-AzureStorageFileContent -Share $share -Source C:\
   Files\MyFile.txt -Path TextFiles
   ```

6. Use the `Get-AzureStorageFile` cmdlet (`PS C:\> Get-AzureStorageFile -Share $share -Path TextFiles`) to list the files in the directory (similar to executing the `dir` or `ls` commands), as shown in the following screenshot:

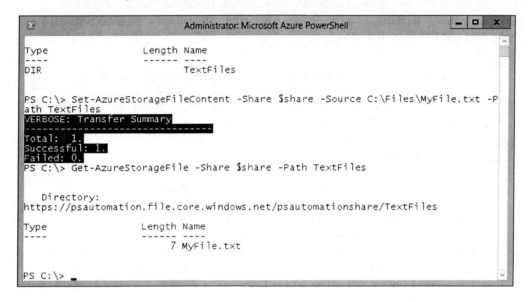

For more information about Microsoft Azure File storage and the cmdlets used in this section, refer to the following resources:

*   How to use Azure File storage (`http://azure.microsoft.com/en-us/documentation/articles/storage-dotnet-how-to-use-files/`)

*   The `Get-AzureStorageFile` cmdlet (`http://msdn.microsoft.com/en-us/library/dn806383.aspx`)

*   The `Set-AzureStorageFileContent` cmdlet (`http://msdn.microsoft.com/en-us/library/dn806404.aspx`)

*   The `Set-Content` cmdlet (`http://technet.microsoft.com/en-us/library/hh849828.aspx`)

*   The `New-AzureStorageDirectory` cmdlet (`http://msdn.microsoft.com/en-us/library/dn806385.aspx`)

*   The `New-AzureStorageShare` cmdlet (`http://msdn.microsoft.com/en-us/library/dn806378.aspx`)

*   The `New-AzureStorageContext` cmdlet (`http://msdn.microsoft.com/en-us/library/dn806380.aspx`)

Using Azure Blog storage

As mentioned in the *Azure File storage versus Azure Blob storage* section, Azure Blob storage can be used to store any unstructured data, including file content. Blobs are stored within containers and permissions are set at the container level. The permission levels that can be assigned to a container are shown in the following table:

Permission level	Access provided
Container	This provides anonymous read access to the container and all blobs in the container. In addition, it allows anonymous users to list the blobs in the container.
Blob	This provides anonymous read access to blobs within the container. Anonymous users cannot list all of the blobs in the container.
Off	This does not provide anonymous access. It is only accessible with the Azure storage account keys.

To illustrate Azure Blob storage, we will use the following steps to create a public container, upload a file, and access the file from a web browser:

1. In the PowerShell session from the *Getting Azure storage account keys* section in which we obtained an access key, use the `New-AzureStorageContext` cmdlet to connect to the Azure storage account and assign it to a variable. Note that the first parameter is the name of the storage account, whereas the second parameter is the access key:

    ```
    PS C:\> $context = New-AzureStorageContext psautomation $key
    ```

2. Use the `New-AzureStorageContainer` cmdlet to create a new public container. Note that the name must contain only numbers and lowercase letters. No special characters, spaces, or uppercase letters are permitted:

    ```
    PS C:\> New-AzureStorageContainer -Name textfiles -Context
    $context -Permission Container
    ```

3. Before uploading a file to the newly created directory, we need to ensure that we have a file to upload. To create a sample file, we can use the `Set-Content` cmdlet to create a new text file:

    ```
    PS C:\> Set-Content C:\Files\MyFile.txt -Value "Hello"
    ```

4. Upload a file using the `Set-AzureStorageBlobContent` cmdlet:

    ```
    PS C:\> Set-AzureStorageBlobContent -File C:\Files\MyFile.txt
    -Blob "MyFile.txt" -Container textfiles -Context $context
    ```

5. Navigate to the newly uploaded blob in Internet Explorer. The URL for the blob is formatted as `https://<StorageAccountName>.blob.core.windows.net/<ContainerName>/<BlobName>`. In our example, the URL is `https://psautomation.blob.core.windows.net/textfiles/MyFile.txt`, as shown in the following screenshot:

For more information about Microsoft Azure Blob storage and the cmdlets used in this section, refer to the following resources:

- How to use Blob storage from .NET (`http://azure.microsoft.com/en-us/documentation/articles/storage-dotnet-how-to-use-blobs/`)

- The `Set-Content` cmdlet (`http://technet.microsoft.com/en-us/library/hh849828.aspx`)

- The `New-AzureStorageContainer` cmdlet (`http://msdn.microsoft.com/en-us/library/dn806381.aspx`)

- The `Set-AzureStorageBlobContent` cmdlet (`http://msdn.microsoft.com/en-us/library/dn806379.aspx`)

- The `New-AzureStorageContext` cmdlet (`http://msdn.microsoft.com/en-us/library/dn806380.aspx`)

Using Azure Table storage

Azure Table storage is useful for storing large amounts of non-relational structured data. Non-relational data refers to data stored in tables (such as SQL databases); however, the tables have no relationship to each other; for instance, there are no foreign key constraints. The service is a NoSQL data store.

The components of Azure Table storage are shown in the following table:

Component	Purpose
Table	A table is a collection of entities, which closely correlates to a SQL database table. However, unlike a SQL database table, a table in Azure does not enforce a specific schema on the entities. Entities with different sets of properties can be stored in the same table.
Entity	An entity is a collection of properties, which closely correlates to a SQL database row.
Property	A property is a name-value pair, which closely correlates to a SQL database field or column value.

Executing CRUD (create, read, update, and delete) operations for entities in an Azure Table is intended to be completed within an application, such as an ASP.NET website. Microsoft Azure PowerShell provides cmdlets to create and manage tables but not to execute CRUD operations. In this example, we will create a new Azure Table. We will cover how to use .NET to write to a table in the *Using Microsoft Azure storage to back up files* section of this chapter.

To create a new table in Azure, we will use the following steps:

1. In the PowerShell session from the *Getting Azure storage account keys* section in which we obtained an access key, use the `New-AzureStorageContext` cmdlet to connect to the Azure storage account and assign it to a variable. Note that the first parameter is the name of the storage account, whereas the second parameter is the access key:

```
PS C:\> $context = New-AzureStorageContext psautomation $key
```

2. Use the `New-AzureStorageTable` cmdlet to create a new table:

```
PS C:\> New-AzureStorageTable -Name MyTable -Context $context
```

For more information about Microsoft Azure Table storage and the cmdlets used in this section, refer to the following resources:

- The How to use Table Storage from .NET (http://azure.microsoft.com/en-us/documentation/articles/storage-dotnet-how-to-use-tables/)

- The `New-AzureStorageTable` cmdlet (http://msdn.microsoft.com/en-us/library/dn806417.aspx)

- The `New-AzureStorageContext` cmdlet (http://msdn.microsoft.com/en-us/library/dn806380.aspx)

Using Azure Queue storage

Microsoft Azure Queue storage is used to store a large number of messages that can be published or accessed via HTTP and HTTPS. Messages can be up to 64 KB in size.

A couple of common uses of Azure Queue storage include:

- Passing messages between separate applications (such as an Azure Web role and an Azure Worker role)
- Creating a backlog of work for a process to complete

Similar to Azure Table storage, Microsoft Azure PowerShell provides cmdlets to create and manage queues but no cmdlets to add to or read from the queues. In this example, we will create a new queue. We will cover how to use .NET to write to a queue in the *Using Microsoft Azure storage to back up files* section of this chapter.

To create a new queue in Azure, we will use the following steps:

1. In the PowerShell session from the *Getting Azure storage account keys* section in which we obtained an access key, use the `New-AzureStorageContext` cmdlet to connect to the Azure storage account and assign it to a variable. Note that the first parameter is the name of the storage account, whereas the second parameter is the access key:

   ```
   PS C:\> $context = New-AzureStorageContext psautomation $key
   ```

2. Use the `New-AzureStorageQueue` cmdlet to create a new queue:

   ```
   PS C:\> New-AzureStorageQueue -Name "MyQueue" -Context $context
   ```

For more information about Microsoft Azure Queue storage and the cmdlets used in this section, see the following resources:

- How to use Queue storage from .NET (http://azure.microsoft.com/en-us/documentation/articles/storage-dotnet-how-to-use-queues/)
- The `New-AzureStorageQueue` cmdlet (http://msdn.microsoft.com/en-us/library/dn806382.aspx)
- The `New-AzureStorageContext` cmdlet (http://msdn.microsoft.com/en-us/library/dn806380.aspx)

Using Microsoft Azure storage to back up files

In this chapter, we covered the basics of the services offered by a Microsoft Azure storage account. This includes file, blob, table, and queue storage. To illustrate the usefulness of these storage services, we will create a PowerShell script that backs up a folder on the local computer to Azure Blob storage, writes a manifest of the files backed up to Azure Table storage, and sends a message to Azure Queue storage indicating that the backup is complete.

> In this example, we will use .NET in PowerShell to complete Azure Table and Azure Queue operations not exposed by cmdlets. As such, we will need to have the Microsoft Azure SDK for .NET installed. The Microsoft Azure SDK for .NET can be installed with the Microsoft Web Platform Installer or from `http://azure.microsoft.com/en-us/develop/net/`.

To create a backup script that uses Azure Blob, Azure Table, and Azure Queue storage, we will use the following steps:

1. Open Windows PowerShell ISE from the Start menu to create a new PowerShell script.

> A PowerShell script, typically a plaintext file with the `.ps1` file extension, contains a set of PowerShell commands. When it is executed, PowerShell will execute each command in the script in the same manner that the Windows Command Prompt executes a batch file (`.bat` or `.cmd`).

2. Set up the variables that we need to create the rest of the script, including the storage account name and access key, the path of the files to back up, and the location of the Azure SDK. Set the values of the variable to match the configuration of the system the script will run on, as shown here:

```
$azureStorageAccessKey = "<insert your key>"

$azureStorageAccountName = "<insert your account name>"

$pathToCompress = "C:\BackupFiles"

$azureSdkVersion = "v2.5"

$programFilesPath = "C:\Program Files"
```

3. Use the `Add-Type` cmdlet to import the `Microsoft.WindowsAzure.Storage.dll` assembly into the session. Note that we are using the `-ErrorAction SilentlyContinue` parameter to ignore errors, such as the assembly already being loaded into the session:

```
Add-Type -Path ($programFilesPath + "\Microsoft
SDKs\Azure\.NET SDK\" + $azureSdkVersion +
"\ToolsRef\Microsoft.WindowsAzure.Storage.dll") -ErrorAction
SilentlyContinue
```

4. Add the functions to create ZIP files. PowerShell 3.0 does not have built-in cmdlets to create ZIP files. The methods used in this example are taken from http://blogs.msdn.com/b/daiken/archive/2007/02/12/compress-files-with-windows-powershell-then-package-a-windows-vista-sidebar-gadget.aspx. Alternatively, the PowerShell Community Extensions (http://pscx.codeplex.com) include cmdlets to create ZIP files:

```
function New-Zip
{
    param([string]$zipfilename)

    set-content $zipfilename ("PK" + [char]5 + [char]6 +
("$([char]0)" * 18))

    (dir $zipfilename).IsReadOnly = $false
}


function Add-Zip
{
    param([string]$zipfilename)

    if(-not (test-path($zipfilename)))
    {
        set-content $zipfilename ("PK" + [char]5 + [char]6
+ ("$([char]0)" * 18))

        (dir $zipfilename).IsReadOnly = $false
    }


    $shellApplication = new-object -com shell.application


    $zipPackage = $shellApplication.NameSpace($zipfilename)
```

```
foreach($file in $input)
{

    $zipPackage.CopyHere($file.FullName)


    Start-sleep -milliseconds 500

}
}
```

5. Use the Get-ChildItem cmdlet to get the files in the backup directory. In this example, we will exclude subdirectories:

```
$files = Get-ChildItem -Path $pathToCompress | Where-Object {
$_.PsIsContainer -eq $false }
```

6. Use the methods we added in step 4 to create a ZIP file that contains the files from the backup directory. Note that we are using the Get-Date cmdlet to use the current date and time to create a unique file name, and we are using the $pwd session variable to get the current directory:

```
$backupDate = Get-Date


$zipName = ("Backup_" +
$backupDate.ToString("yyyy_MM_dd_HH_mm_ss") + ".zip")


$zipPath = [System.IO.Path]::Combine($pwd.Path, $zipName)


New-Zip $zipPath


$files | Add-Zip $zipPath
```

7. Use the New-AzureStorageContext cmdlet to open a new connection in the Azure storage account:

```
$context = New-AzureStorageContext $azureStorageAccountName
$azureStorageAccessKey
```

8. Use the Get-AzureStorageContainer cmdlet to get the Azure Blob storage container to add the ZIP file. If it does not already exist, use the New-AzureStorageContainer cmdlet to create it. Note that PowerShell uses operators, such as -eq, -gt, -lt, and -neq, for comparisons rather than code operators (such as ==, >, <, and !=):

```
$container = Get-AzureStorageContainer -Name backups -
Context $context -ErrorAction SilentlyContinue
```

```
if ($container -eq $null)

{

    $container = New-AzureStorageContainer -Name backups -
Context $context -Permission Off

}
```

9. Use the `Set-AzureBlobStorageContent` cmdlet to upload the ZIP file to Azure Blob storage:

```
Set-AzureStorageBlobContent -File $zipPath -Blob $zipName -
Container backups -Context $context
```

10. Use the `Get-AzureStorageTable` cmdlet to get the Azure Table to store the file backup records. If the table does not exist, use the `New-AzureStorageTable` cmdlet to create it:

```
$table = Get-AzureStorageTable backuprecords -Context
$context -ErrorAction SilentlyContinue


if ($table -eq $null)

{

    $table = New-AzureStorageTable backuprecords -Context
$context

}
```

11. For each file backup, create a new `DynamicTableEntity` object using the `New-Object` cmdlet and insert it into the table. Note that we are assigning the result of the insert operation to a variable. Although we are not making use of it in this example, this variable could be used to determine the success or failure of the operation:

```
$row = 0


foreach ($file in $files)

{

    $filePath = $file.FullName


    $entity = New-Object
Microsoft.WindowsAzure.Storage.Table.DynamicTableEntity -
ArgumentList $zipName, $row


    $entity.Properties.Add("BackupDate", [String]
$backupDate.ToString())
```

```
$entity.Properties.Add("BackupZip", [String] $zipName)


$entity.Properties.Add("FilePath", [String] $filePath)


$result =
$table.CloudTable.Execute([Microsoft.WindowsAzure.Storage.T
able.TableOperation]::Insert($entity))


$row = $row + 1
}
```

> Using the New-Object cmdlet in this context to instantiate
> a .NET object is the equivalent of creating var entity
> = new Microsoft.WindowsAzure.Storage.Table.
> DynamicTableEntity(zipName, row); in C#. With PowerShell
> built-in .NET, we can translate any .NET code into PowerShell
> commands and can access any .NET class or function that we could
> translate with .NET code.

12. Use the Get-AzureStorageQueue cmdlet to get the Azure Queue to
    send a message to. If the queue does not already exist, use the New-
    AzureStorageQueue cmdlet to create it:

```
$queue = Get-AzureStorageQueue backupqueue -Context $context -
ErrorAction SilentlyContinue


if ($queue -eq $null)
{
    $queue = New-AzureStorageQueue backupqueue -Context
$context
}
```

13. Use the New-Object cmdlet to create a new CloudQueueMessage object to
    send to the queue:

```
$messageString = ("Backup '" + $zipName + "' completed. " +
$files.Count.ToString() + " files backed up.");


$message = New-Object
Microsoft.WindowsAzure.Storage.Queue.CloudQueueMessage -
ArgumentList $messageString
```

14. Send this message to the queue:

    ```
    $queue.CloudQueue.AddMessage($message)
    ```

15. Save the PowerShell script with the name `BackupFiles.ps1` for example.

16. Open Microsoft Azure PowerShell from the Start menu. Note that, as we already have the storage account name and access key, we do not actually need to connect to Azure with Active Directory credentials or a publish settings file.

17. Execute the backup script (`PS C:\> .\BackupFiles.ps1`), as shown in the following screenshot:

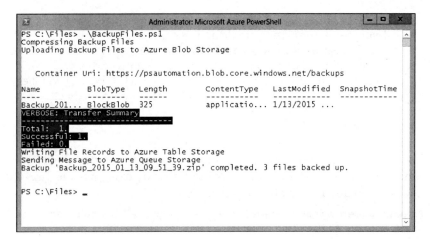

For this example, a complete copy of the script is included in the sample code of this book. The complete script includes commands to output the current operation to the console window.

Using these techniques, we could take this example further and create processes that occur after a message has been sent to the Azure Queue. For instance, we could have a service that takes the details of the backup from the queued message and the Azure Table storage to e-mail someone the details of the backup or any errors that might occur in the process.

For more information about the techniques and cmdlets used in this section, refer to the following resources:

- Azure SDK for .NET (`http://azure.microsoft.com/en-us/develop/net/`)
- The `Add-Type` cmdlet (`http://technet.microsoft.com/en-us/library/hh849914.aspx`)

- Compress files with Windows PowerShell (`http://blogs.msdn.com/b/daiken/archive/2007/02/12/compress-files-with-windows-powershell-then-package-a-windows-vista-sidebar-gadget.aspx`)

- PowerShell Community Extensions (`http://pscx.codeplex.com`)

- The `Get-ChildItem` cmdlet (`http://technet.microsoft.com/en-us/library/hh849800.aspx`)

- The `Get-Date` cmdlet (`http://technet.microsoft.com/en-us/library/hh849887.aspx`)

- The `New-Object` cmdlet (`http://technet.microsoft.com/en-us/library/hh849885.aspx`)

Summary

In this chapter, you learned about Microsoft Azure storage accounts and how to interact with storage account services with PowerShell. This included file storage, blob storage, table storage, and queue storage. In addition, we applied this knowledge by creating a script that backs up a folder to blob storage, writes the details to table storage, and sends a message to queue storage. With a little bit of planning, these techniques can be incorporated in a variety of business applications and processes.

Imagine a payroll processing company that receives payroll data from hundreds of companies and then processes them in multiple, geographically-separate data centers to spread the load and act as a fail-safe in the event a data center goes offline. The customers could submit encrypted employee data to blob storage and send a message to queue storage indicating that a payroll batch is ready to process. The payroll company's processing applications take the next item in the queue, retrieve the blob, and complete the payroll processing. Lastly, the payroll company could then send paystubs to blob storage, payroll details to table storage, and a message indicating the processing is complete to queue storage.

Similar to many Microsoft Azure services, storage accounts provide powerful tools that can be included in solutions that solve real business needs and improve antiquated business processes.

In the next chapter, we will explore how to create and manage virtual machines in Microsoft Azure.

3

Managing Azure Virtual Machines with PowerShell

A **virtual machine (VM)** is an emulation of a computer system that allows an operating system to run virtually inside the operating system installed on a computer. Microsoft's implementation of virtual machine technologies is Hyper-V. Hyper-V is available as a standalone server product called Hyper-V Server, as an installable role in Windows 8 (64-bit) and newer client operating systems, and as an installable role in Windows Server 2008 and newer server operating systems.

Virtual machines are incredibly useful for maximizing the utilization of available computing power, and what can be afforded. For instance, let's say an organization requires four servers for their operations for these purposes: Microsoft Exchange, Microsoft SharePoint, Microsoft SQL Server, and Microsoft Active Directory. The company could choose to purchase and maintain four physical servers. However, to reduce the costs involved (including the cost of the hardware, electricity, and so on) and to utilize the hardware in a better way (by not having a server with a lot of unused hardware resources such as CPU and memory), it could choose to use Hyper-V. The company could use one or two physical servers with the four servers required running in virtual machines.

In addition to reducing the amount of physical hardware required and cost savings, virtual machines are also incredibly useful in development and testing scenarios. For instance, when testing changes to an environment, snapshots can be used to save the state of a virtual machine prior to making the change. In the event the change needs to be reverted, the virtual machine simply gets reverted back to the snapshot.

Although virtual machines are great at reducing costs and maximizing hardware utilization, Microsoft Azure virtual machines can be used without any hardware costs at all. They can also be accessed from anywhere in the world.

Virtual machines in Microsoft Azure

One of the first and most useful services offered by Microsoft Azure is virtual machine hosting. Microsoft Azure virtual machines run on servers in the cloud as part of Azure and do not require any hardware on the part of the customer. The virtual disks and images for Azure virtual machines are stored using Microsoft Azure blob storage, whereas virtual machines run in Hyper-V on Azure servers.

There are three key components to be aware of with Microsoft Azure virtual machines: instances, images, and disks. Azure virtual machine instances define and run the virtual machine. Configuration details, such as the amount of memory and number of CPU cores, are defined as part of the virtual machine instance.

When creating new virtual machines, images in Microsoft Azure virtual machines provide the template for the virtual disk. For instance, an image can include Microsoft Windows Server 2012 R2 and Microsoft SQL Server 2014. When a new virtual machine is created using an image, the new virtual machine will copy this image and configure it for the virtual machine.

Microsoft Azure includes a number of images that are ready to use. The images include various versions of Windows Server, various Microsoft server products (such as SQL, Exchange, and SharePoint), and a number of preconfigured images using non-Microsoft operating systems (such as Linux). In addition, you can create your own images in Hyper-V and upload them to Microsoft Azure.

> To use your own virtual disk as an image, you must run `sysprep` for Windows-based machines or run `waagent -deprovision` for Linux-based machines to prepare it as an image. For more information on preparing image templates for Azure virtual machines, refer to `http://blogs.technet.com/b/keithmayer/archive/2013/01/17/step-by-step-templating-vms-in-the-cloud-with-windows-azure-and-powershell-31-days-of-servers-in-the-cloud-part-17-of-31.aspx`.

Lastly, Microsoft Azure virtual machines use virtual disks (`.vhd` files) stored in Azure blob storage. When creating a new Azure virtual machine from an image, these disks are generated automatically in the process. In addition, if you are migrating a virtual machine to Azure, you can upload the virtual disk to Azure blob storage and use it while creating a new virtual machine.

In this chapter, we will explore how to create and manage virtual machines in Microsoft Azure. Note that we will cover how to connect to Azure virtual machines via the **Remote Desktop Protocol (RDP)** in *Chapter 8, Managing Azure Cloud Services with PowerShell*.

For more information about virtual machines, Hyper-V, and Microsoft Azure virtual machines, refer to the following resources:

- Hyper-V overview (`http://technet.microsoft.com/library/hh831531.aspx`)
- Hyper-V (`http://en.wikipedia.org/wiki/Hyper-V`)
- Virtual machine (`http://en.wikipedia.org/wiki/Virtual_machine`)
- Microsoft Azure virtual machines (`http://azure.microsoft.com/en-us/services/virtual-machines/`)

Creating a Microsoft Azure virtual machine

Creating new Microsoft Azure virtual machines is a relatively easy process. We will first select a virtual machine image to use and then create the virtual machine.

Selecting a virtual machine image

As creating new virtual machine images or templates is outside the scope of this book, we are going to work with the existing images provided by Microsoft Azure to create a virtual machine. To retrieve a list of available virtual machine images, we will use the following steps:

1. Open Microsoft Azure PowerShell from the Start menu and connect it to an Azure subscription.

 We must first be connected to Azure in order to create and manage virtual machines. If not connected to Azure, refer to the *Connecting to a Microsoft Azure subscription* section in *Chapter 1, Getting Started with Azure and PowerShell*.

2. Use the `Get-AzureVMImage` cmdlet to list the available images. Note that we are using the `Where-Object` cmdlet to limit the results in order to display only Windows Server 2012 R2 datacenter images, and we are using the `Format-List` cmdlet to display only the name of the image (`ImageName`) and its description (`Label`). There are hundreds of images available in Microsoft Azure; limiting the results helps us to narrow down what we are looking for:

```
PS C:\> Get-AzureVMImage | Where-Object { $_.Label -Match
"Windows Server 2012 R2 Datacenter" } | Format-List -Property
ImageName,Label
```

There are a variety of ways in which we can filter the available images to find what we are looking for. For instance, using `Get-AzureVMImage | Select-Object Label,OS,PublisherName` will list all the images with their title, operating system, and the organization that published the image to Microsoft Azure.

3. Make a note of `ImageName` for the virtual machine image that we will use when creating a new virtual machine in the next section, *Creating a virtual machine*:

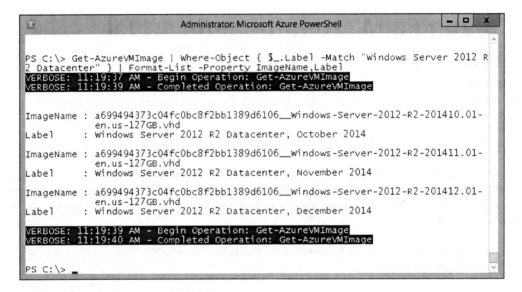

For more information about the cmdlets used in this example, use the `Get-Help` cmdlet in PowerShell, or refer to the following resources:

- The `Get-AzureVMImage` cmdlet (`http://msdn.microsoft.com/en-us/library/azure/dn495275.aspx`)

- The `Where-Object` cmdlet (`http://technet.microsoft.com/en-us/library/hh849715.aspx`)

- The `Format-List` cmdlet (`http://technet.microsoft.com/en-us/library/hh849957.aspx`)

Creating a virtual machine

Having chosen an `ImageName` in the *Selecting a virtual machine image* section, we can now create a new Microsoft Azure virtual machine instance.

> When creating an Azure virtual machine, we will need to select a size. The size of an Azure virtual machine dictates the amount of memory provided and the number of CPU cores. The larger the size, the more expensive the virtual machine will be to run. Refer to `http://msdn.microsoft.com/library/azure/dn197896.aspx` for the list of available sizes for Microsoft Azure virtual machines. In this example, we will use `Small`, which provides 1.75 GB of memory and 1 CPU core.

We will use the following steps to create a new Microsoft Azure virtual machine instance:

1. Open Microsoft Azure PowerShell from the Start menu and connect it to an Azure subscription.

> We must first be connected to Azure in order to create and manage virtual machines. If not connected to Azure, refer to the *Connecting to a Microsoft Azure subscription* section in *Chapter 1, Getting Started with Azure and PowerShell*.

2. Use the `New-AzureQuickVM` cmdlet (`PS C:\> New-AzureQuickVM -Windows -ServiceName "PSAutomation2012R2" -Name "PSAuto2012R2" -Location "West US" -AdminUsername "PSAutomation" -Password "Pa$$w0rd" -InstanceSize "Small" -ImageName "a699494373c04fc0bc8f2bb1389d6106__Windows-Server-2012-R2-201412.01-en.us-127GB.vhd"`) to create a new virtual machine instance with the `ImageName` chosen in the *Selecting a virtual machine image* section. Note that we set the initial administrator username and password for the virtual machine:

In this example, we will use `West US` as the data center location for the new virtual machine. To retrieve a full list of available locations to choose from, use the `Get-AzureLocation` cmdlet. For example, `Get-AzureLocation | Select-Object Name` will list only the names of the locations.

When creating the new Azure virtual machine, an Azure cloud service is also automatically provisioned for the virtual machine. This is used to connect to the virtual machine, which we will cover in *Chapter 8, Managing Azure Cloud Services with PowerShell*.

For more information about the cmdlets used in this section, use the `Get-Help` cmdlet in PowerShell, or refer to the following resources:

- The `New-AzureQuickVM` cmdlet (http://msdn.microsoft.com/en-us/library/azure/dn495183.aspx)

- The `Get-AzureLocation` cmdlet (http://msdn.microsoft.com/en-us/library/azure/dn495177.aspx)

- The `Select-Object` cmdlet (http://technet.microsoft.com/en-us/library/hh849895.aspx)

Managing Microsoft Azure virtual machines

Once Microsoft Azure virtual machines have been created, there are a number of ways in which we can manage them with PowerShell. This includes starting, stopping, and removing virtual machines. In addition, we will create a new virtual disk and attach it to a virtual machine instance.

Listing the instances of Microsoft Azure virtual machines

The first action we will take is to get a list of the virtual machine instances currently in our Microsoft Azure subscription. We will see the name of the virtual machine, the name of the cloud service associated with the virtual machine, and the provisioning status of the instance. Secondly, we will check the power state of the virtual machines. The power state indicates whether the virtual machine instance is running or turned off. To complete these actions, we will use the following steps:

1. Open Microsoft Azure PowerShell from the Start menu and connect it to an Azure subscription.

 We must first be connected to Azure in order to manage virtual machines. If not connected to Azure, refer to the *Connecting to a Microsoft Azure subscription* section in *Chapter 1, Getting Started with Azure and PowerShell*.

2. Use the Get-AzureVM cmdlet (PS C:\> Get-AzureVM) without any parameters to list the virtual machine instances. Note that a ReadyRole status means that the virtual machine has been provisioned and is ready for use:

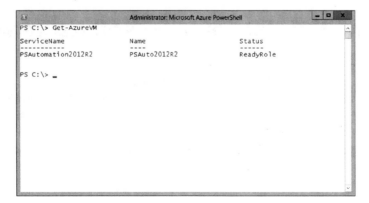

3. Use the `Get-AzureVM` and `Select-Object` cmdlets (`PS C:\> Get-AzureVM | Select-Object Name,PowerState`) to retrieve the list of virtual machine instances and display the power states of the virtual machines:

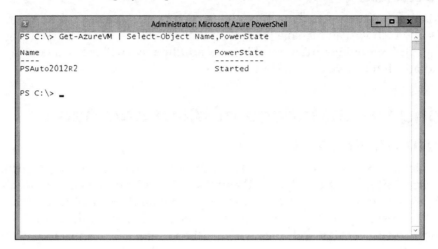

```
Administrator: Microsoft Azure PowerShell                    _  □  X
PS C:\> Get-AzureVM | Select-Object Name,PowerState

Name                              PowerState
----                              ----------
PSAuto2012R2                      Started

PS C:\> _
```

4. Assign a virtual machine to a PowerShell variable for use in the *Managing the state of Microsoft Azure virtual machine instances* section:

```
PS C:\> $vm = Get-AzureVM –Name "PSAuto2012R2" –ServiceName
"PSAutomation2012R2"
```

For more information about the cmdlets used in this section, use the `Get-Help` cmdlet in PowerShell, or refer to the following resources:

- The `Get-AzureVM` cmdlet (`http://msdn.microsoft.com/en-us/library/azure/dn495236.aspx`)

- The `Select-Object` cmdlet (`http://technet.microsoft.com/en-us/library/hh849895.aspx`)

Managing the state of Microsoft Azure virtual machine instances

With instances of Microsoft Azure virtual machines, we can start, stop, and restart them. Starting an Azure virtual machine essentially turns on the virtual machine, while stopping it essentially turns off the virtual machine. Also, restarting a virtual machine essentially reboots a virtual machine. Unlike virtual machines in your own instance of Hyper-V, Microsoft Azure virtual machines cannot be paused.

Before you continue, be sure that you have a virtual machine assigned to a PowerShell variable, as described earlier in the *Listing the instances of Microsoft Azure virtual machines* section.

To restart, stop, and start a virtual machine in Microsoft Azure, we will use the following steps:

1. Use the `Restart-AzureVM` cmdlet to restart the virtual machine instance:

    ```
    PS C:\> Restart-AzureVM -Name $vm.Name -ServiceName
    $vm.ServiceName
    ```

2. Use the `Stop-AzureVM` cmdlet to stop the virtual machine instance. Note that, when you stop a virtual machine instance, its deployment network configuration (including its IP addresses) will be discarded. To keep the current IP addresses, the `-StayProvisioned` parameter can be used:

    ```
    PS C:\> Stop-AzureVM -Name $vm.Name -ServiceName
    $vm.ServiceName
    ```

3. Use the `Start-AzureVM` cmdlet to start the virtual machine instance:

    ```
    PS C:\> Start-AzureVM -Name $vm.Name -ServiceName
    $vm.ServiceName
    ```

For more information about the cmdlets used in this section, use the `Get-Help` cmdlet in PowerShell, or refer to the following resources:

*   The `Restart-AzureVM` cmdlet (`http://msdn.microsoft.com/en-us/library/azure/dn495199.aspx`)

*   The `Stop-AzureVM` cmdlet (`http://msdn.microsoft.com/en-us/library/azure/dn495269.aspx`)

*   The `Start-AzureVM` cmdlet (`http://msdn.microsoft.com/en-us/library/azure/dn495226.aspx`)

Creating a snapshot of a Microsoft Azure virtual machine instance

Microsoft Azure virtual machines do not offer a simple snapshot feature like having your own instance of Hyper-V server does. However, we can create a copy of the `.vhd` virtual disk file used by the virtual machine instance in Azure blob storage. This essentially allows you to create a backup or snapshot of the virtual machine instance.

Before you continue, be sure that you have a virtual machine assigned to a PowerShell variable, as described in the *Listing the instances of Microsoft Azure virtual machines* section.

To create a snapshot or backup of a Microsoft Azure virtual machine instance, we will use the following steps:

1. Display the URL of the blob for the `.vhd` virtual disk file of the virtual machine instance (`PS C:\> $vm.VM.OSVirtualHardDisk`):

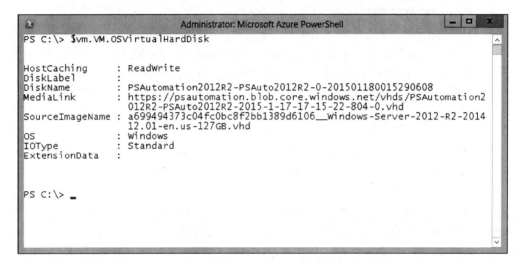

2. Use the `Get-AzureStorageBlob` cmdlet to retrieve the blob record for the `.vhd` virtual disk file and assign it to a variable. The names of the container and blob are present in the `MediaLink` property (as shown in the previous step):

   ```
   PS C:\> $blob = Get-AzureStorageBlob –Container "vhds" –Blob
   "PSAutomation2012R2-PSAuto2012R2-2015-1-17-17-15-22-804-0.vhd"
   ```

3. Open the blob so that it can be read:

   ```
   PS C:\> $blob.ICloudBlob.OpenRead()
   ```

4. Use the `Start-AzureStorageBlobCopy` cmdlet (`PS C:\> Start-AzureStorageBlobCopy -ICloudBlob $blob.ICloudBlob -DestContainer "vhds" -DestBlob "PSAutomation2012R2-PSAuto2012R2-2015-1-17-17-15-22-804-0.vhd_Snapshot-2015-01-18" -DestContext $blob.Context`) to copy the blob of the `.vhd` virtual disk file. Specify a name that makes sense for a snapshot, such as appending the word "snapshot" and the date to the original filename:

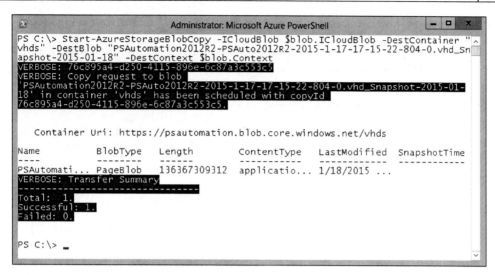

```
PS C:\> Start-AzureStorageBlobCopy -ICloudBlob $blob.ICloudBlob -DestContainer "
vhds" -DestBlob "PSAutomation2012R2-PSAuto2012R2-2015-1-17-17-15-22-804-0.vhd_Sn
apshot-2015-01-18" -DestContext $blob.Context
VERBOSE: 76c895a4-d250-4115-896e-6c87a3c553c5
VERBOSE: Copy request to blob
'PSAutomation2012R2-PSAuto2012R2-2015-1-17-17-15-22-804-0.vhd_Snapshot-2015-01-
18' in container 'vhds' has been scheduled with copyId
76c895a4-d250-4115-896e-6c87a3c553c5.


   Container Uri: https://psautomation.blob.core.windows.net/vhds

Name            BlobType    Length         ContentType    LastModified  SnapshotTime
----            --------    ------         -----------    ------------  ------------
PSAutomati...   PageBlob    136367309312   applicatio...  1/18/2015 ...
VERBOSE: Transfer Summary
--------------------------------
Total:      1.
Successful: 1.
Failed:     0.


PS C:\> _
```

 Another method to back up (or create a snapshot of) a virtual disk is to use Azure blob storage snapshots. After getting the blob record in step 2, the command `$blob.ICloudBlob.CreateSnapshot()` will create a snapshot of the `.vhd` file using blob storage snapshots:

For more information about the cmdlets used in this section, use the `Get-Help` cmdlet in PowerShell, or refer to the following resources:

- The `Start-AzureStorageBlobCopy` cmdlet (http://msdn.microsoft.com/en-us/library/dn806394.aspx)
- The `Get-AzureStorageBlob` cmdlet (http://msdn.microsoft.com/en-us/library/dn806392.aspx)

Creating a new virtual disk and assigning it to a Microsoft Azure virtual machine instance

Virtual disks act like hard drives to virtual machines. In this section, we will create a new virtual disk and assign it to an Azure virtual machine instance. Afterwards, we will remove the data disk.

 Before you continue, be sure that you have a virtual machine assigned to a PowerShell variable, as described in the *Listing the instances of Microsoft Azure virtual machines* section.

To create, assign, and remove a virtual data disk, we will use the following steps:

1. Use the `Add-AzureDataDisk` and `Update-AzureVM` cmdlets to create a new virtual disk and attach it to the virtual machine instance:

   ```
   PS C:\> Add-AzureDataDisk -CreateNew -DiskSizeInGB 10 -
   DiskLabel "DataDisk" -VM $vm -LUN 0 | Update-AzureVM
   ```

2. Use the `Get-AzureDataDisk` cmdlet (`PS C:\> Get-AzureDataDisk -VM $vm`) to view the virtual data disks associated with the Azure virtual machine instance:

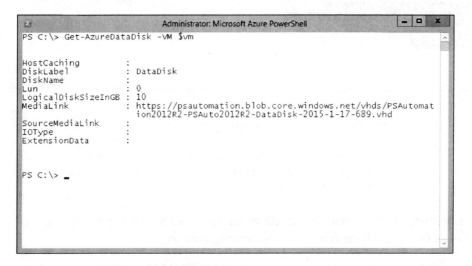

3. Use the `Remove-AzureDataDisk` and `Update-AzureVM` cmdlets to remove the virtual data disk from the Azure virtual machine instance and delete the `.vhd` file for the virtual disk. If you want to keep the `.vhd` file for the virtual disk, exclude the `-DeleteVHD` parameter:

   ```
   PS C:\> Remove-AzureDataDisk –LUN 0 –VM $vm –DeleteVHD |
   Update-AzureVM
   ```

For more information about the cmdlets used in this section, use the `Get-Help` cmdlet in PowerShell, or refer to the following resources:

- The `Add-AzureDataDisk` cmdlet (`http://msdn.microsoft.com/en-us/library/azure/dn495298.aspx`)

- The `Remove-AzureDataDisk` cmdlet (`http://msdn.microsoft.com/en-us/library/azure/dn495243.aspx`)

- The `Update-AzureVM` cmdlet (http://msdn.microsoft.com/en-us/library/azure/dn495230.aspx)

- The `Get-AzureDataDisk` cmdlet (http://msdn.microsoft.com/en-us/library/azure/dn495197.aspx)

Removing a Microsoft Azure virtual machine instance

Once a Microsoft Azure virtual machine is no longer needed, it's good practice to remove the virtual machine. This prevents any potential future subscription fees and can free up space in an Azure storage account.

 Before you continue, be sure that you have a virtual machine assigned to a PowerShell variable, as described in the *Listing the instances of Microsoft Azure virtual machines* section.

To remove a Microsoft Azure virtual machine instance, we will use the following steps:

1. Use the `Remove-AzureVM` cmdlet to delete the virtual machine instance. Use the `-DeleteVHD` parameter if you would also like to delete the `.vhd` virtual disk file associated with the virtual machine. If you would like to keep the virtual disk file, exclude the `-DeleteVHD` parameter. In the event that you need to use this virtual machine again, this allows you to create a new virtual machine using this virtual disk:

```
PS C:\> Remove-AzureVM –Name $vm.Name –ServiceName
$vm.ServiceName
```

2. Use the `Get-AzureVM` cmdlet (`PS C:\> Get-AzureVM`) to verify that the virtual machine instance no longer exists:

For more information about the cmdlets used in this section, use the `Get-Help` cmdlet in PowerShell, or refer to the following resources:

- The `Remove-AzureVM` cmdlet (`http://msdn.microsoft.com/en-us/library/azure/dn495199.aspx`)

- The `Get-AzureVM` cmdlet (`http://msdn.microsoft.com/en-us/library/azure/dn495236.aspx`)

Downloading the example code

You can download the example code files for all Packt books you have purchased from your account at `http://www.packtpub.com`. If you purchased this book elsewhere, you can visit `http://www.packtpub.com/support` and register to have the files e-mailed directly to you.

Summary

In this chapter, you learned about Microsoft Azure virtual machines. This includes creating, managing, and removing virtual machine instances. In addition, you learned about creating and removing virtual disks for virtual machine instances. Connecting to Microsoft Azure virtual machines with Microsoft Azure cloud services will be covered in *Chapter 8, Managing Azure Cloud Services with PowerShell*. In the next chapter, we will explore how to manage Azure SQL databases.

4
Managing Azure SQL Databases with PowerShell

In *Chapter 2*, *Managing Azure Storage with PowerShell*, we explored Azure Table storage that allows us to store non-relational data entities. While table storage is useful to store records with no related data, many enterprise applications require much more complex data storage. SQL databases, such as Microsoft SQL Server and Microsoft Azure SQL Database, provide complex data storage structures required by these applications.

Microsoft Azure SQL Databases provide most of the functionality of an instance of Microsoft SQL Server using the same syntax (T-SQL) and methodologies. While there are a few key limitations (refer to the references at the end of this section), Azure SQL Databases provide simplified management of SQL databases. In addition, Azure SQL Databases allow for geo-replication and other redundancy or high-availability features that allow organizations to scale databases globally without the need to have their own data centers globally.

In this chapter, we will explore how to manage Microsoft Azure SQL Databases using PowerShell. This includes managing SQL servers, SQL databases, and firewall rules. In addition, we will connect to an Azure SQL Database to perform queries against it.

 Microsoft Azure virtual machines provide another way to host SQL databases in Microsoft Azure. This method might be the best solution depending on the requirements of an application. However, in this chapter, we will cover Microsoft Azure SQL databases.

For more information about SQL databases and Azure SQL databases, refer to the following resources:

- Comparison of SQL Server with Azure SQL Database (`http://social.technet.microsoft.com/wiki/contents/articles/996.comparison-of-sql-server-with-azure-sql-database.aspx`)
- Azure SQL Database Transact-SQL reference (`http://msdn.microsoft.com/en-us/library/ee336281.aspx`)
- Microsoft Azure SQL Database (`http://azure.microsoft.com/en-us/services/sql-database/`)

Creating and connecting to Microsoft Azure SQL Database Servers

Similar to Microsoft SQL Server Databases, SQL Databases in Microsoft Azure are hosted by Microsoft Azure SQL Database Servers. Before creating any SQL Databases, we must first have a database server and access to it. In this section, we will create a new Microsoft Azure SQL Database Server and a firewall rule that allows us to connect to it. In addition, we will create a connection context for the database server, which allows us to create and manage databases in the sections to follow.

Provisioning a new Microsoft Azure SQL Database Server

To create a new Microsoft Azure SQL Database Server instance, we will use the following steps:

1. Open Microsoft Azure PowerShell from the Start menu and connect it to an Azure subscription.

> We must first be connected to Azure in order to work with Microsoft Azure SQL. If not connected to Azure, refer to the *Connecting to a Microsoft Azure subscription* section in *Chapter 1, Getting Started with Azure and PowerShell*.

2. Use the `New-AzureSqlDatabaseServer` cmdlet (`PS C:\> New-AzureSqlDatabaseServer -Location "West US" -AdministratorLogin "PSAutomation" -AdministratorLoginPassword "P@$$w0rd"`) to create the new Azure SQL Database Server. The administrator username and password provided in the command will be used to create a new SQL account that has administrator privileges (note that `sa` cannot be used):

> In this example, we will use `West US` as the data center location for the new virtual machine. To retrieve a full list of available locations to choose from, use the `Get-AzureLocation` cmdlet. For example, `Get-AzureLocation | Select-Object Name` will list only the names of the locations.

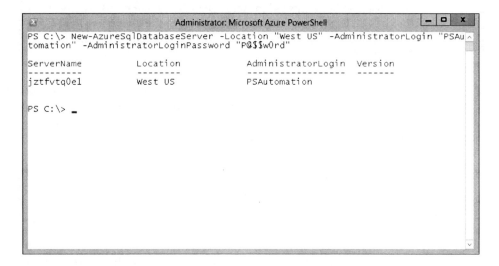

3. Make a note of the `ServerName` value returned. We will use this in the sections to follow.

For more information about the cmdlets used in this section, use the `Get-Help` cmdlet in PowerShell, or refer to the following resources:

- The `New-AzureSqlDatabaseServer` cmdlet (http://msdn.microsoft.com/en-us/library/dn546730.aspx)

- The `Get-AzureLocation` cmdlet (http://msdn.microsoft.com/en-us/library/azure/dn495177.aspx)

- The `Select-Object` cmdlet (http://technet.microsoft.com/en-us/library/hh849895.aspx)

Configuring a firewall rule for a Microsoft Azure SQL Database server

By default, only other Microsoft Azure services are allowed through the firewall for a Microsoft Azure SQL Database instance. To connect to a SQL database server from outside Azure, such as from your local computer, a firewall rule needs to be added for your public IP address. We will use the following steps to create a new firewall rule for the database server that we created in the *Provisioning a new Microsoft Azure SQL Database Server* section:

1. Open Microsoft Azure PowerShell from the Start menu and connect it to an Azure subscription.

> We must first be connected to Azure in order to work with Microsoft Azure SQL. If not connected to Azure, refer to the *Connecting to a Microsoft Azure subscription* section in *Chapter 1, Getting Started with Azure and PowerShell*.

2. Obtain the public IP address you would like to add to the firewall. If you do not know what your public IP address is, search on Google.com or Bing.com for your IP address. Both search engines will return your current public IP address at the beginning of the search results.

> We could add all possible IP addresses to the firewall rule. However, doing so would essentially leave your database server without the protection the firewall offers.

3. Use the New-AzureSqlDatabaseServerFirewallRule cmdlet to create a new firewall rule on the SQL database server for the public IP address from the previous step. For a single IP address, the IP address acts as both the starting and ending IP address for the firewall rule:

```
PS C:\> New-AzureSqlDatabaseServerFirewallRule -RuleName
"MyIPAddress" -ServerName "jztfvtq0el" -StartIpAddress
123.123.123.123 -EndIpAddress 123.123.123.123
```

> If you need to retrieve the name of the Azure SQL Database Server, use the Get-AzureSqlDatabase cmdlet to list the names of the servers in the current Azure subscription.

For more information about the cmdlets used in this section, use the `Get-Help` cmdlet in PowerShell, or refer to the following resources:

- The `Get-AzureSqlDatabase` cmdlet (http://msdn.microsoft.com/en-us/library/dn546735.aspx)

- The `New-AzureSqlDatabaseFirewallRule` cmdlet (http://msdn.microsoft.com/en-us/library/dn546724.aspx)

Connecting to a Microsoft Azure SQL Database Server with PowerShell

With a new Microsoft Azure SQL Database Server created and a firewall rule added, we can now connect to the database server. We will use the following steps to connect to the database server:

1. Open Microsoft Azure PowerShell from the Start menu and connect it to an Azure subscription.

 We must first be connected to Azure in order to work with Microsoft Azure SQL. If not connected to Azure, refer to the *Connecting to a Microsoft Azure subscription* section in *Chapter 1, Getting Started with Azure and PowerShell*.

2. Assign the SQL database administrator credentials (the username and password used in the *Provisioning a new Microsoft Azure SQL Database Server* section) to a PowerShell variable using the `Get-Credential` cmdlet (PS C:\> $credentials = Get-Credential):

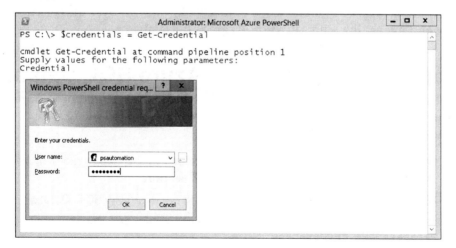

3. Use the `New-AzureSqlDatabaseServerContext` cmdlet to create a new connection to the SQL database server and assign the connection context to a PowerShell variable:

```
PS C:\> $context = New-AzureSqlDatabaseServerContext -
ServerName "jztfvtq0el" -Credential $credentials
```

 If you need to retrieve the name of the Azure SQL Database Server, use the `Get-AzureSqlDatabase` cmdlet to list the names of the servers in the current Azure subscription.

For more information about the cmdlets used in this section, use the `Get-Help` cmdlet in PowerShell, or refer to the following resources:

- The `New-AzureSqlDatabaseServerContext` cmdlet (http://msdn. microsoft.com/en-us/library/dn546736.aspx)

- The `Get-AzureSqlDatabase` cmdlet (http://msdn.microsoft.com/en-us/ library/dn546735.aspx)

- The `Get-Credential` cmdlet (http://technet.microsoft.com/en-us/ library/hh849815.aspx)

Creating and managing Microsoft Azure SQL Databases

Microsoft Azure SQL Databases provide a wide variety of capabilities to store and manage relational data. While developing SQL databases (including tables and stored procedures) is outside the scope of this book, we will cover the basics of creating and interacting with Microsoft Azure SQL Databases.

Creating a new Microsoft Azure SQL Database

A SQL Database is the hierarchical container in which tables, stored procedures, functions, and other SQL objects are stored. We will use the following steps to create a new Microsoft Azure SQL Database:

1. Create a new connection context, as described in the *Connecting to a Microsoft Azure SQL Database Server with PowerShell* section.

2. Use the `New-AzureSqlDatabase` cmdlet to create a new SQL Database:

```
PS C:\> New-AzureSqlDatabase –ConnectionContext $context -
DatabaseName "MyDatabase"
```

3. Use the `Get-AzureSqlDatabase` cmdlet (`PS C:\> Get-AzureSqlDatabase -ConnectionContext $context`) to verify the results of creating the SQL Database:

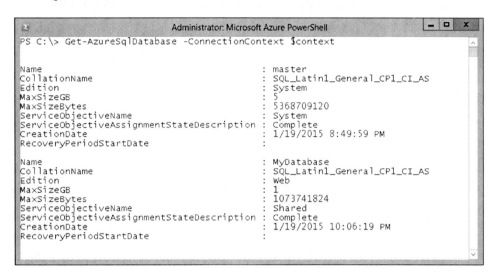

```
Administrator: Microsoft Azure PowerShell                        -  □  x
PS C:\> Get-AzureSqlDatabase -ConnectionContext $context

Name                                     : master
CollationName                            : SQL_Latin1_General_CP1_CI_AS
Edition                                  : System
MaxSizeGB                                : 5
MaxSizeBytes                             : 5368709120
ServiceObjectiveName                     : System
ServiceObjectiveAssignmentStateDescription : Complete
CreationDate                             : 1/19/2015 8:49:59 PM
RecoveryPeriodStartDate                  :

Name                                     : MyDatabase
CollationName                            : SQL_Latin1_General_CP1_CI_AS
Edition                                  : Web
MaxSizeGB                                : 1
MaxSizeBytes                             : 1073741824
ServiceObjectiveName                     : Shared
ServiceObjectiveAssignmentStateDescription : Complete
CreationDate                             : 1/19/2015 10:06:19 PM
RecoveryPeriodStartDate                  :
```

For more information about the cmdlets used in this section, use the `Get-Help` cmdlet in PowerShell, or refer to the following resources:

- The `Get-AzureSqlDatabase` cmdlet (`http://msdn.microsoft.com/en-us/library/dn546735.aspx`)

- The `New-AzureSqlDatabase` cmdlet (`http://msdn.microsoft.com/en-us/library/dn546722.aspx`)

Executing queries with a Microsoft Azure SQL Database

Microsoft Azure PowerShell does not include cmdlets to interact with Microsoft Azure SQL Database tables directly. However, as PowerShell is built on the .NET Framework, we can use .NET code to execute queries in PowerShell.

Before completing this section, we should have the Microsoft Azure SQL Database we created in the *Creating a new Microsoft Azure SQL Database* section.

We will use the following steps to create a simple SQL database table, insert a record, and query the record:

1. Open Microsoft Azure PowerShell or Windows PowerShell from the Start menu.

     In this example, as we are only using .NET methods to interact with the Microsoft Azure SQL Database, Microsoft Azure PowerShell can be used but is not required.

2. Assign the connection string for the Microsoft Azure SQL Database to a PowerShell variable. The connection string for .NET to connect to a Microsoft Azure SQL Database is formatted as `Server=tcp:<Server Name>.database.windows.net,1433;Database=<Database Name>;User ID=<User Name>@<Server Name>;Password=<Password>;Trusted_Conn ection=False;Encrypt=True;Connection Timeout=30;`. It includes the server name (twice), the database name, the username, and the password:

    ```
    PS C:\> $connectionString =
    "Server=tcp:jztfvtq0e1.database.windows.net,1433;Database=MyDa
    tabase;User ID=PSAutomation@jztfvtq0e1;
    Password=P@$$w0rd;Trusted_Connection=False;Encrypt=True;
    Connection Timeout=30;"
    ```

3. Use the `New-Object` cmdlet to create a new `SqlConnection` object and open this SQL connection:

    ```
    PS C:\> $connection = New-Object
    System.Data.SqlClient.SqlConnection -ArgumentList
    $connectionString

    PS C:\> $connection.Open()
    ```

4. Use the `New-Object` cmdlet to create a new `SqlCommand` object, and execute a SQL query to create a new SQL table:

    ```
    PS C:\> $command = New-Object System.Data.SqlClient.SqlCommand

    PS C:\> $command.CommandText = "CREATE TABLE [dbo].[MyData]
    ([RecordID] INT NOT NULL PRIMARY KEY IDENTITY(1,1), [MyValue]
    NVARCHAR(MAX) NOT NULL)"

    PS C:\> $command.Connection = $connection

    PS C:\> $command.ExecuteNonQuery()
    ```

5. Use the `New-Object` cmdlet to create a new `SqlCommand` object and execute a SQL query to insert a new row in the table, as created in the previous step:

```
PS C:\> $command = New-Object System.Data.SqlClient.SqlCommand
PS C:\> $command.CommandText = "INSERT [dbo].[MyData]
([MyValue]) VALUES ('Hello')"
PS C:\> $command.Connection = $connection
PS C:\> $command.ExecuteNonQuery()
```

6. Use the `New-Object` cmdlet to create new `DataTable` and `SqlDataAdapter` objects and execute a SQL query to select the row created in the previous step:

```
PS C:\> $result = New-Object System.Data.DataTable
PS C:\> $adapter = New-Object
System.Data.SqlClient.SqlDataAdapter -ArgumentList "SELECT *
FROM [dbo].[MyData]",$connection
PS C:\> $adapter.Fill($result)
```

7. Output the results of the SQL query from the previous step by entering the `$result` variable (`PS C:\> $result`):

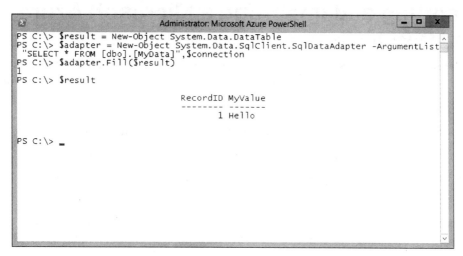

8. Close the database connection:

```
PS C:\> $connection.Close()
```

For more information about the cmdlet and .NET classes used in this section, refer to the following resources:

- The `New-Object` cmdlet (http://technet.microsoft.com/en-us/library/hh849885.aspx)

- The `System.Data.SqlClient.SqlConnection` class (http://msdn.microsoft.com/en-us/library/system.data.sqlclient.sqlconnection(v=vs.110).aspx)

- The `System.Data.SqlClient.SqlCommand` class (http://msdn.microsoft.com/en-us/library/system.data.sqlclient.sqlcommand(v=vs.110).aspx)

- The `System.Data.SqlClient.SqlDataAdapter` class (http://msdn.microsoft.com/en-us/library/system.data.sqlclient.sqldataadapter(v=vs.110).aspx)

- The `System.Data.DataTable` class (http://msdn.microsoft.com/en-us/library/system.data.datatable(v=vs.110).aspx)

Exporting and importing a Microsoft Azure SQL Database

With applications that use SQL databases, there are a number of common scenarios in which a SQL Database needs to be copied or backed up. A few examples include:

- Scheduling backups or snapshots of a database

- Copying a database from a staging to a production environment

- Saving the state of a database prior to making structural changes

- Making a copy of a production database to troubleshoot or investigate in a non-production environment

Microsoft Azure Blob storage is used when exporting and importing Microsoft Azure SQL Databases. We will use the following steps to export a database and import it into a new database:

1. Create a new connection context, as described in the *Connecting to a Microsoft Azure SQL Database Server with PowerShell* section.

 Before we continue, we should have a database available; we created one in the *Creating and managing Microsoft Azure SQL Databases* section.

2. Use the `Get-AzureStorageKey` and `New-AzureStorageContext` cmdlets to create a new Microsoft Azure storage account context and assign it to a variable. Refer to *Chapter 2, Managing Azure Storage with PowerShell*, for more information about creating and connecting to an Azure storage account:

```
PS C:\> $accountKey = Get-AzureStorageKey –StorageAccountName
psautomation

PS C:\> $storageContext = New-AzureStorageContext psautomation
$accountKey.Primary
```

3. Use the `New-AzureStorageContainer` cmdlet to create a new Azure Blob storage container for the SQL Database export:

```
PS C:\> $container = New-AzureStorageContainer –Name
sqlexports –Context $storageContext –Permission Off
```

4. Export the SQL Database using the `Start-AzureSqlDatabaseExport` cmdlet and assign the following request to a variable:

```
PS C:\> $request = Start-AzureSqlDatabaseExport –
SqlConnectionContext $context –StorageContainer $container –
DatabaseName "MyDatabase" –BlobName
"MyDatabaseExport_2015_01_20"
```

5. Use the `Get-AzureSqlDatabaseImportExportStatus` cmdlet to check the status of the export. Once the export is complete, continue to the next step:

```
PS C:\> Get-AzureSqlDatabaseImportExportStatus –Request
$request
```

6. Use the `Start-AzureSqlDatabaseImport` cmdlet to import the database into a new SQL Database. By providing a database name that does not already exist, a new one will be created automatically:

```
PS C:\> Start-AzureSqlDatabaseImport –SqlConnectionContext
$context –StorageContainer $container –DatabaseName
"MyDatabaseImported" –BlobName "MyDatabaseExport_2015_01_20"
```

For more information about importing and exporting Microsoft Azure SQL Databases and the cmdlets used in this section, refer to the following resources:

- Operations for Azure SQL Databases (http://msdn.microsoft.com/en-us/library/dn505719.aspx)

- The `Get-AzureStorageKey` cmdlet (http://msdn.microsoft.com/en-us/library/azure/dn495235.aspx)

- The `New-AzureStorageContext` cmdlet (http://msdn.microsoft.com/en-us/library/dn806380.aspx)

- The New-AzureStorageContainer cmdlet (http://msdn.microsoft.com/en-us/library/dn806381.aspx)
- The Start-AzureSqlDatabaseExport cmdlet (http://msdn.microsoft.com/en-us/library/dn546720.aspx)
- The Get-AzureSqlDatabaseImportExportStatus cmdlet (http://msdn.microsoft.com/en-us/library/dn546734.aspx)
- The Start-AzureSqlDatabaseImport cmdlet (http://msdn.microsoft.com/en-us/library/dn546725.aspx)

Removing a Microsoft Azure SQL Database

As with most Microsoft Azure services, the last part of the life cycle of a Microsoft Azure SQL Database is to remove it. This prevents any future charges for the database and removes it completely from Microsoft Azure. To remove the SQL Database we created in the *Creating a new Microsoft Azure SQL Database* section, we will use the following steps:

1. Create a new connection context, as described in the *Connecting to a Microsoft Azure SQL Database Server with PowerShell* section.

2. Use the Remove-AzureSqlDatabase cmdlet to delete the database from the Microsoft Azure SQL Database Server instance:

   ```
   PS C:\> Remove-AzureSqlDatabase -ServerName "jztfvtq0e1" -
   DatabaseName "MyDatabase"
   ```

For more information about the Remove-AzureSqlDatabase cmdlet, use the Get-Help cmdlet in PowerShell, or refer to http://msdn.microsoft.com/en-us/library/dn546741.aspx.

Summary

Microsoft Azure SQL Databases are a powerful and effective way to store and manage large amounts of relational data in the cloud. In this chapter, you learned how to create and manage Microsoft Azure SQL Database Servers and Microsoft Azure SQL Databases. In addition, you learned how to connect to and interact with SQL data in PowerShell.

In the next chapter, you will learn how to create, deploy, and manage Microsoft Azure websites using PowerShell.

5
Deploying and Managing Azure Websites with PowerShell

The Internet live stats site (http://www.internetlivestats.com/) reports that, in September 2014, the Internet reached a milestone of over 1 billion active websites. One or more web servers host each of these websites. While some individuals and organizations host websites on their own servers, many choose to rely on hosting services provided by one of thousands of web hosting providers.

In addition to the network of global data centers, Microsoft Azure offers web hosting services that include many features that are not found elsewhere. Some features of Azure web hosting include:

- Support for common languages and frameworks, including .NET, Java, PHP, and Python
- Database hosting, including Microsoft SQL, MySQL, and MongoDB
- Support for popular web applications, including WordPress, Drupal, and DotNetNuke
- One-click deployment from Visual Studio
- Continuous deployment from Git and Team Foundation Server
- Automatic scaling based on load or schedules

In this chapter, we will cover the basics of creating and managing Microsoft Azure websites with PowerShell. For more information about Microsoft Azure web hosting, refer to http://azure.microsoft.com/en-us/services/websites/.

Creating and configuring a new Microsoft Azure website

Microsoft Azure websites offer a variety of configuration options, such as the version of .NET, the version of PHP, application settings, and logging. To create and configure a new website, we will use the following steps:

1. Open Microsoft Azure PowerShell from the Start menu and connect it to an Azure subscription.

    We must first be connected to Azure in order to work with Microsoft Azure websites. If not connected to Azure, refer to the *Connecting to a Microsoft Azure subscription* section in *Chapter 1, Getting Started with Azure and PowerShell*.

2. Use the `New-AzureWebsite` cmdlet to create a new Microsoft Azure website. The name provided will be used to create the initial domain name and must be unique. For instance, `psautomation` will result in the initial domain name of `psautomation.azurewebsites.net`:

    ```
    PS C:\> New-AzureWebsite –Name psautomation –Location "West
    US"
    ```

    In this example, we will use `West US` as the data center location for the new website. To retrieve a full list of available locations to choose from, use the `Get-AzureLocation` cmdlet. For example, `Get-AzureLocation | Select-Object Name` will list only the names of the locations.

3. Use the `Get-AzureWebsite` cmdlet (`PS C:\> Get-AzureWebsite –Name psautomation | Select-Object HostNames`) to retrieve the hostname or domain name of the newly created website:

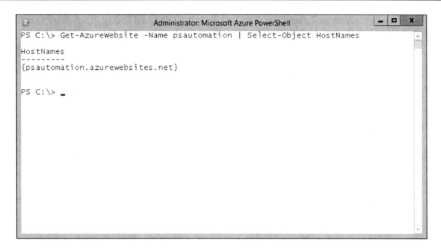

4. Navigate to the newly created website in Internet Explorer.

 You can navigate to the website manually in the Internet Explorer or use the Show-AzureWebsite cmdlet to do it automatically, for example, Show-AzureWebsite -Name psautomation.

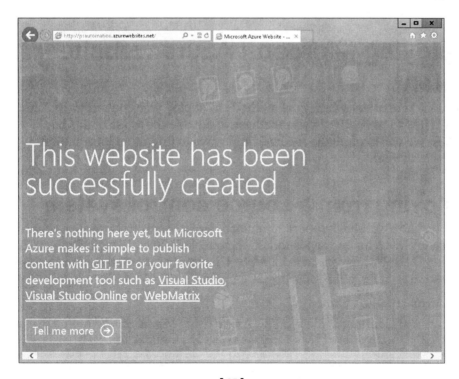

5. Use the `Set-AzureWebsite` cmdlet to enable HTTP logging and configure app settings to store Azure storage account access information:

```
PS C:\> $appSettings = New-Object Hashtable
PS C:\> $appSettings["StorageKey"] = "<Storage Account Key>"
PS C:\> $appSettings["StorageName"] = "psautomation"
PS C:\> Set-AzureWebsite –Name psautomation –
HttpLoggingEnabled 1 –AppSettings $appSettings
```

For more information about Microsoft Azure websites and the cmdlets used in this example, refer to the following resources:

- The `Set-AzureWebsite` cmdlet (https://msdn.microsoft.com/en-us/library/azure/dn495207.aspx)
- The `Get-AzureWebsite` cmdlet (https://msdn.microsoft.com/en-us/library/azure/dn495127.aspx)
- The `New-AzureWebsite` cmdlet (https://msdn.microsoft.com/en-us/library/azure/dn495157.aspx)
- The `Show-AzureWebsite` cmdlet (https://msdn.microsoft.com/en-us/library/azure/dn495153.aspx)
- Microsoft Azure websites and apps (http://azure.microsoft.com/en-us/services/websites/)

Deploying Microsoft Azure website content

Microsoft Azure offers a variety of methods to deploy web content to an Azure website. How to use each of these methods is outside the scope of this book. However, we will explore the methods and ways to find more information about each method.

Deploying from a source control system

Microsoft Azure websites support automated deployments from various cloud-based source control systems and repositories. These include Visual Studio Online, Git (including GitHub), Mercurial, and Dropbox. For more information about using each of these sources, refer to the following resources:

- Visual Studio online:
  - Continuous delivery to Azure using Visual Studio online (http://azure.microsoft.com/en-us/documentation/articles/cloud-services-continuous-delivery-use-vso/)

- Continuous delivery to Azure using Visual Studio online and Git (`http://azure.microsoft.com/en-us/documentation/articles/cloud-services-continuous-delivery-use-vso-git/`)

- Git and Mercurial:
  - Publishing to Azure websites with Git (`http://azure.microsoft.com/en-us/documentation/articles/web-sites-publish-source-control/`)

- Dropbox:
  - Deploy to Windows Azure websites from Dropbox (`http://azure.microsoft.com/blog/2013/03/19/new-deploy-to-windows-azure-web-sites-from-dropbox/`)

Deploying from Visual Studio or WebMatrix

Microsoft Visual Studio (the 2012 version and higher) and Microsoft WebMatrix (version 2 and higher) support one-click deployments to Microsoft Azure websites. For more information about deploying to Azure websites with these development tools, refer to the following resources:

- Get started with Azure websites and ASP.NET for Visual Studio (`http://azure.microsoft.com/en-us/documentation/articles/web-sites-dotnet-get-started/`)
- Develop and deploy a website with Microsoft WebMatrix (`http://azure.microsoft.com/en-us/documentation/articles/web-sites-dotnet-using-webmatrix/`)

Other deployment methods

In addition to deploying from source control, Visual Studio, or WebMatrix, content can be deployed with FTP and various command-line tools. For a complete list of all the available methods, refer to **How to Deploy an Azure Website** (`http://azure.microsoft.com/en-us/documentation/articles/web-sites-deploy/`).

Managing Microsoft Azure websites

Beyond creating and configuring Microsoft Azure websites, common management tasks for Azure websites include checking the status of websites, gathering website logs, starting and stopping websites, and removing websites. We will use the following steps to complete these tasks, using the website we created in the *Creating and configuring a new Microsoft Azure website* section:

1. Open Microsoft Azure PowerShell from the Start menu and connect it to an Azure subscription.

    We must first be connected to Azure in order to work with Microsoft Azure websites. If not connected to Azure, refer to the *Connecting to a Microsoft Azure subscription* section in *Chapter 1, Getting Started with Azure and PowerShell*.

2. Use the Get-AzureWebsite cmdlet (PS C:\> Get-AzureWebsite) to list the websites in the current Azure subscription and display the status of each:

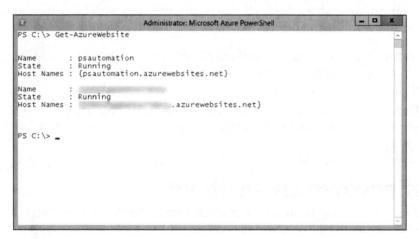

3. Use the Get-AzureWebsiteLog cmdlet (PS C:\> Get-AzureWebsiteLog -Name psautomation -Path http -Tail) to stream log entries from the website to the PowerShell window. The log entries returned are directly from **Internet Information Services (IIS)** that run the website in Azure. This will run until you press the *Ctrl* and *C* keys at the same time to exit the command. Note that, after pressing *Ctrl* + *C*, it might take up to a minute for the command to exit:

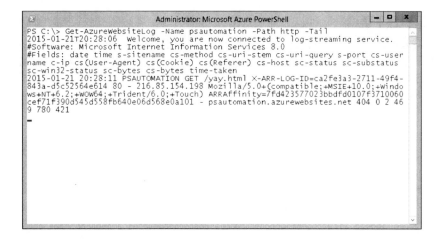

```
PS C:\> Get-AzureWebsiteLog -Name psautomation -Path http -Tail
2015-01-21T20:28:06  Welcome, you are now connected to log-streaming service.
#Software: Microsoft Internet Information Services 8.0
#Fields: date time s-sitename cs-method cs-uri-stem cs-uri-query s-port cs-user
name c-ip cs(User-Agent) cs(Cookie) cs(Referer) cs-host sc-status sc-substatus
sc-win32-status sc-bytes cs-bytes time-taken
2015-01-21 20:28:11 PSAUTOMATION GET /yay.html X-ARR-LOG-ID=ca2fe3a3-2711-49f4-
843a-d5c52564e614 80 - 216.85.154.198 Mozilla/5.0+(compatible;+MSIE+10.0;+Windo
ws+NT+6.2;+WOW64;+Trident/6.0;+Touch) ARRAffinity=7fd423577023bbdfd0107f3710060
cef71f390d545d558fb640e06d568e0a101 - psautomation.azurewebsites.net 404 0 2 46
9 780 421
```

4. Use the `Stop-AzureWebsite` cmdlet to stop the website. This results in the website no longer being served up by the IIS instance that runs the website in Azure:

   PS C:\> Stop-AzureWebsite psautomation

5. Use the `Start-AzureWebsite` cmdlet to start the website. Performing a stop and start of a website is essentially the same thing as restarting IIS on a local web server:

   PS C:\> Start-AzureWebsite psautomation

6. Use the `Remove-AzureWebsite` cmdlet to remove the website from Microsoft Azure. This will permanently remove the website and stop any recurring subscription fees for the website:

   PS C:\> Remove-AzureWebsite psautomation

For more information about the cmdlets used in this section, use the `Get-Help` cmdlet in PowerShell, or refer to the following resources:

- The `Remove-AzureWebsite` cmdlet (https://msdn.microsoft.com/en-us/library/azure/dn495151.aspx)

- The `Start-AzureWebsite` cmdlet (https://msdn.microsoft.com/en-us/library/azure/dn495288.aspx)

- The `Stop-AzureWebsite` cmdlet (https://msdn.microsoft.com/en-us/library/azure/dn495185.aspx)

- The `Get-AzureWebsite` cmdlet (https://msdn.microsoft.com/en-us/library/azure/dn495127.aspx)

- The `Get-AzureWebsiteLog` cmdlet (https://msdn.microsoft.com/en-us/library/azure/dn495187.aspx)

Summary

In this chapter, we covered creating, configuring, and managing websites in Microsoft Azure. In addition, you learned about the various methods available to publish content to Microsoft Azure websites. In the next chapter, we will explore managing Microsoft Azure virtual networks.

6
Managing Azure Virtual Networks with PowerShell

Microsoft Azure Virtual Network is a network overlay that allows Azure virtual machines and services to communicate with each other while preventing services outside the virtual network for accessing them. Virtual networks or VNets also allow you to connect between the Azure Virtual Network and an organization's local on-premise network.

There are three types of virtual networks that can be configured for Microsoft Azure services:

- **No virtual network**: This is the default configuration for Microsoft Azure services. The services are not connected to any virtual network and operate as an isolated service. For instance, Azure virtual machines will not have any access to any other Azure virtual machines by default.

- **Cloud-only virtual network**: This network exists only within Microsoft Azure and allows any services within the virtual network to communicate with each other as if they were on the same physical network.

- **Cross-premises virtual network**: This network extends an organization's local on-premise network to an Azure Virtual Network. This allows computers and services within the networks to communicate with each other as if they were on the same physical network.

Cross-premises virtual networks provide three types of connectivity between an Azure Virtual Network and an organization's network:

- **Site-to-site VPN**: This VPN creates a secure connection between an on-premise network and a virtual network. The site-to-site VPN uses a VPN device in the on-premise network that connects to the Azure Virtual Network gateway in the cloud. The connection is created over the Internet.

- **Point-to-site VPN**: This VPN creates a secure connection between an individual client computer and the virtual network. The connection is created over the Internet.

- **ExpressRoute**: This uses a direct connection between the on-premise network and a Microsoft Azure data center. The direct connection is typically provided by a third-party service provider and does not use the Internet for the connection. ExpressRoute is the most expensive option. However, it allows you to have a more secure connection between the on-premise network and virtual network. In addition, the bandwidth available is much greater than using one of the VPN options. This option is typically only used for organizations that have a large on-premise network and a large implementation of Microsoft Azure services.

Private virtual networks in Microsoft Azure can only use valid private IPv4 addresses. The ranges of these IP addresses include: `10.0.0.0 - 10.255.255.255`, `172.16.0.0 - 172.31.255.255`, and `192.168.0.0 - 192.168.255.255`.

In this chapter, we will explore how to create and manage cloud-only virtual networks. In addition, we will create an Azure virtual machine and assign it to the new virtual network. Configuring hybrid virtual networks requires advanced networking configuration on an organization's local network, which is outside the scope of this book.

For more information about Microsoft Azure Virtual Network, refer to the following resources:

- Microsoft Azure Virtual Network (`http://azure.microsoft.com/en-us/services/virtual-network/`)

- Microsoft Azure Virtual Network overview (`https://msdn.microsoft.com/library/azure/jj156007.aspx`)

- Microsoft Azure About Secure Cross-Premises Connectivity (`https://msdn.microsoft.com/en-us/library/azure/dn133798.aspx`)

- Microsoft Azure Virtual Network FAQ (`https://msdn.microsoft.com/library/azure/dn133803.aspx`)

Creating and managing an Azure Virtual Network

To create a new Azure Virtual Network, we must first create a network configuration file. After we have created a configuration file, we can create the virtual network. Then, we create new virtual machines in the virtual network.

Creating an Azure Virtual Network configuration file

An Azure Virtual Network file provides details about the virtual network. It is in XML format and can include the elements shown in the following table:

Element name	Required	Description
DnsServer	No	This specifies the Domain Name Servers for the virtual network (up to nine). If no DNS servers are provided, the default Azure DNS servers will be used.
LocalNetworkSite	No	This specifies information about local (on-premise) network sites associated with the virtual network (up to 10).
VPNGatewayAddress	No	This specifies the VPN tunnels used between local (on-premise) network sites and the virtual network.
AddressPrefix (LocalNetworkSite)	No	This specifies the address space for the local (on-premise) network site.
VirtualNetworkSite	Yes	This specifies the name and location (or affinity group) of the virtual network.
Gateway	No	This specifies the gateway used for cross-premises connections from the virtual network.
AddressPrefix (Gateway)	No	This specifies the address space for VPN clients.
LocalNetworkSiteRef (Gateway)	No	This specifies the external networks to connect to the gateway.
Connection (Gateway)	No	This specifies the type of local (on-premise) network site.
VirtualNetworkSiteRef	No	This specifies another virtual network the virtual network can communicate with.
DnsServerRef	Yes	This specifies which of the DNS servers are used for the virtual network.
Subnet	Yes	This specifies the subnets within the address space of the virtual network.
AddressPrefix (Subnet)	Yes	This specifies the address space for a subnet.
AddressPrefix (VirtualNetworkSite)	Yes	This specifies the address space for a virtual network.

For this example, we will use the following steps to create a configuration file:

1. Open Notepad from the Start menu (or any plain text editor) to create the new configuration file.

2. Add the following configuration data:

```xml
<?xml version="1.0" encoding="utf-8"?>
<NetworkConfiguration xmlns="http://schemas.microsoft.com/
ServiceHosting/2011/07/NetworkConfiguration">
  <VirtualNetworkConfiguration>
    <Dns>
      <DnsServers>
        <DnsServer name="DNS1" IPAddress="10.10.1.1"/>
      </DnsServers>
    </Dns>
    <VirtualNetworkSites>
      <VirtualNetworkSite name="PSAutomation"
Location="West US">
        <DnsServersRef>
          <DnsServerRef name="DNS1"/>
        </DnsServersRef>
        <Subnets>
          <Subnet name="SubProxyServer">
            <AddressPrefix>10.10.2.32/27</AddressPrefix>
          </Subnet>
        </Subnets>
        <AddressSpace>
          <AddressPrefix>10.10.1.0/16</AddressPrefix>
        </AddressSpace>
      </VirtualNetworkSite>
    </VirtualNetworkSites>
  </VirtualNetworkConfiguration>
</NetworkConfiguration>
```

3. Save the file as an XML file, for instance, `C:\Files\VNetConfig.xml`.

In this example, the configuration file creates a new virtual network called `PSAutomation` with `10.10.1.1` as the DNS server, `10.10.1.0/16` as the address space, and a subnet with `10.10.2.32/27` as the address space.

> A single configuration file is used for each Azure subscription to define up to 10 virtual networks. To change an existing virtual network configuration, update the existing configuration file rather than create a new one.

Computer networking concepts, such as DNS servers and subnets, are outside the scope of this book. For more information about computer networking and Azure Virtual Network configuration, refer to the following resources:

- Computer network (`http://en.wikipedia.org/wiki/Computer_network`)
- Understanding TCP/IP addressing and subnetting (`http://support2.microsoft.com/kb/164015`)
- Microsoft Azure Virtual Network Overview: (`https://msdn.microsoft.com/library/azure/jj156007.aspx`)
- Microsoft Azure Virtual Network Configuration Schema (`https://msdn.microsoft.com/library/azure/jj157100`)

Creating an Azure Virtual Network

With the configuration file created in the *Creating an Azure Virtual Network configuration file* section, we can now create the Azure Virtual Network. We will use the following steps to create a new Azure Virtual Network:

1. Open Microsoft Azure PowerShell from the Start menu and connect it to an Azure subscription.

 We must first be connected to Azure in order to work with Microsoft Azure Virtual Network instances. If not connected to Azure, refer to the *Connecting to a Microsoft Azure subscription* section in *Chapter 1, Getting Started with Azure and PowerShell*.

2. Use the `Set-AzureVNetConfig` cmdlet to upload the configuration file and create the Azure Virtual Network:

```
PS C:\> Set-AzureVNetConfig -ConfigurationPath
C:\Files\VNetConfig.xml
```

3. Use the `Get-AzureVNetSite` cmdlet (`PS C:\> Get-AzureVNetSite`) to verify that the virtual network site we defined in the configuration file was created:

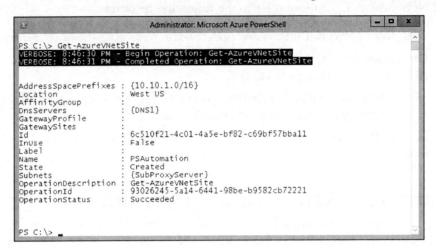

For more information about the cmdlets used in this section, use the `Get-Help` cmdlet in PowerShell, or refer to the following resources:

- The `Get-AzureVNetSite` cmdlet (`https://msdn.microsoft.com/en-us/library/azure/dn495238.aspx`)

- The `Set-AzureVNetConfig` cmdlet (`https://msdn.microsoft.com/en-us/library/azure/dn495195.aspx`)

Creating virtual machines in an Azure Virtual Network

With an Azure Virtual Network in place, we can create new virtual machines in the virtual network. We will use the methods from the *Creating a Microsoft Azure virtual machine* section in *Chapter 3*, *Managing Azure Virtual Machines with PowerShell*.

We will use the following steps to create a new virtual machine in a virtual network:

1. Open Microsoft Azure PowerShell from the Start menu and connect it to an Azure subscription.

We must first be connected to Azure in order to work with Microsoft Azure Virtual Network instances. If not connected to Azure, refer to the *Connecting to a Microsoft Azure subscription* section in *Chapter 1*, *Getting Started with Azure and PowerShell*.

2. Use the `New-AzureQuickVM` cmdlet to create a new virtual machine. Set the `-VNetName` parameter to associate the new virtual machine with the virtual network:

```
PS C:\> New-AzureQuickVM -VNetName PSAutomation -Windows -
ServiceName "PSAutomation2012R2VNet" -Name "PSVNet2012R2" -
Location "West US" -AdminUsername "PSAutomation" -Password
"Pa$$w0rd" -InstanceSize "Small" -ImageName
"a699494373c04fc0bc8f2bb1389d6106__Windows-Server-2012-R2-
201412.01-en.us-127GB.vhd"
```

> For more information about how to create an Azure virtual machine, refer to the *Creating a Microsoft Azure virtual machine* section in *Chapter 3, Managing Azure Virtual Machines with PowerShell*.

Backing up an Azure Virtual Network configuration

When making changes to a Microsoft Azure Virtual Network configuration, it's good practice to make a copy of the existing configuration in case it needs to be reverted to a previous state. In addition, using the backed up network configuration file will provide a starting point from which to make future changes to the virtual network configuration.

We will use the following steps to back up an Azure Virtual Network configuration file:

1. Open Microsoft Azure PowerShell from the Start menu and connect it to an Azure subscription.

> We must first be connected to Azure in order to work with Microsoft Azure Virtual Network instances. If not connected to Azure, refer to the *Connecting to a Microsoft Azure subscription* section in *Chapter 1, Getting Started with Azure and PowerShell*.

2. Use the `Get-AzureVNetConfig` cmdlet with the `-ExportToFile` parameter to export the existing virtual network configuration and save it as a file:

```
PS C:\> Get-AzureVNetConfig -ExportToFile C:\Files\Backup.xml
```

For more information about the `Get-AzureVNetConfig` cmdlet, use the `Get-Help` cmdlet in PowerShell, or refer to https://msdn.microsoft.com/en-us/library/azure/dn495309.aspx.

Removing an Azure Virtual Network configuration

When virtual networks are no longer needed in a Microsoft Azure subscription, we can remove the Azure Virtual Network configuration altogether. However, if we remove an individual virtual network while leaving others in place, we should edit the existing Azure Virtual Network configuration rather than remove it.

We will use the following steps to remove an Azure Virtual Network configuration from an Azure subscription:

1. Open Microsoft Azure PowerShell from the Start menu and connect it to an Azure subscription.

> We must first be connected to Azure in order to work with Microsoft Azure Virtual Network instances. If not connected to Azure, refer to the *Connecting to a Microsoft Azure subscription* section in *Chapter 1, Getting Started with Azure and PowerShell*.

2. Use the `Remove-AzureVNetConfig` cmdlet to remove the Azure Virtual Network configuration from the Azure subscription:

```
PS C:\> Remove-AzureVNetConfig
```

For more information about the `Remove-AzureVNetConfig` cmdlet, use the `Get-Help` cmdlet in PowerShell, or refer to `https://msdn.microsoft.com/en-us/library/azure/dn495250.aspx`.

Summary

Microsoft Azure Virtual Network provides a comprehensive and powerful mechanism to make Azure virtual machines and services part of an organization's infrastructure. While we did not specifically cover how to connect an on-premise network to Azure, we did cover the different types of virtual networks. In addition, we covered how to create and manage Azure Virtual Network configurations.

In the next chapter, we will explore how to use and manage Microsoft Azure Traffic Manager.

7
Managing Azure Traffic Manager with PowerShell

The Alexa website (http://www.alexa.com/) reports that Bing (http://www.bing.com/) is the 25th most visited website on the Internet (as of January 2015). Bing processes millions of search requests each day. With such a heavy load, it would be impossible for a single web server to handle all of the Bing traffic and search requests. In addition, if Bing became unavailable due to the web server being offline, it would be disastrous in terms of end user experience, and users would choose a different search engine.

Load-balancing web servers allow the loaded website traffic to be spread across multiple web servers. It also allows the load of the website traffic to be spread across multiple, geographically separate data centers. Proper implementation of load balancing allows redundancy if a data center or server goes offline. It also allows web requests to be processed quickly, enhancing the end user experience.

Without load balancing, most major websites on the Internet would be very slow. For many users, they would simply not work. Any organization that relies on a website for its livelihood should consider load-balancing their website to ensure that it almost never goes offline and always provides a fast user experience.

Microsoft Azure Traffic Manager provides load-balancing configuration options for Microsoft Azure websites, cloud services, and other web-based endpoints. Traffic Manager distributes user traffic over multiple locations, including both Azure and on-premise data centers. Traffic can be distributed using three methods:

- **Failover**: This has a primary endpoint for all traffic and uses a backup endpoint when the primary endpoint is unavailable
- **Round-robin**: This has multiple endpoints that distribute the traffic load based on weighted rules
- **Performance**: This has multiple endpoints in different geographic locations, and incoming requests use the data center with the lowest latency

Traffic Manager allows you to use nested configurations. For instance, a large public website could be configured with performance-based load balancing to direct traffic to US-based and Europe-based Azure data centers based on which single location has the lowest latency for a request. For European data centers, failover load balancing could be configured between the North Europe and West Europe data centers. For the US data centers, round-robin load-balancing could be configured between the West US and East US data centers:

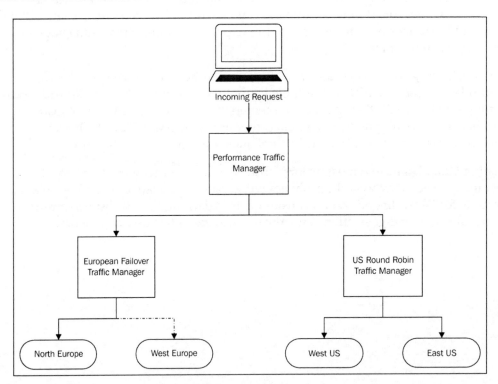

In this chapter, we will create two Microsoft Azure websites, each in a different data center, and use Microsoft Traffic Manager to provide a failover when the primary website is offline. For more information about load balancing and Microsoft Traffic Manager, refer to the following resources:

- Load balancing computing (`http://en.wikipedia.org/wiki/Load_balancing_(computing)`)

- Microsoft Azure Traffic Manager (`http://azure.microsoft.com/en-us/services/traffic-manager/`)

- Microsoft Azure Traffic Manager Overview (`https://msdn.microsoft.com/en-us/library/azure/hh744833.aspx`)

- Microsoft Azure About Traffic Manager Load Balancing Methods (`https://msdn.microsoft.com/en-us/library/azure/dn339010.aspx`)

Creating Microsoft Azure websites for load balancing

In the *Creating and configuring a new Microsoft Azure website* section of *Chapter 5, Deploying and Managing Azure Websites with PowerShell*, we covered how to create a new Microsoft Azure website. We will use that method to create two new Azure websites with the following steps:

1. Open Microsoft Azure PowerShell from the Start menu and connect it to an Azure subscription.

> We must first be connected to Azure in order to work with Microsoft Azure websites. If not connected to Azure, refer to the *Connecting to a Microsoft Azure subscription* section in *Chapter 1, Getting Started with Azure and PowerShell*.

2. Use the `New-AzureWebsite` cmdlet to create a new Microsoft Azure website:

```
PS C:\> New-AzureWebsite -Name psautoprimary -Location "West US"
```

> In this example, we will use `West US` as the data center location for the new website. To retrieve a full list of available locations to choose from, use the `Get-AzureLocation` cmdlet. For example, `Get-AzureLocation | Select-Object Name` will list only the names of the locations.

3. Use the `New-AzureWebsite` cmdlet to create a new Microsoft Azure website with a different name and data center:

   ```
   PS C:\> New-AzureWebsite -Name psautofailover -Location "East
   US"
   ```

4. Use the `Get-AzureWebsite` cmdlet (`PS C:\> Get-AzureWebsite`) to observe the two newly created websites:

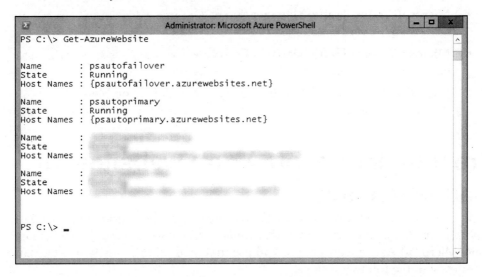

5. Before we can add a Microsoft Azure website to a Traffic Manager profile, we must set the hosting mode to **Standard**. **Free** and **Shared** hosted websites do not support Traffic Manager. We must make this change in the Microsoft Azure management portal. Navigate to `https://manage.windowsazure.com` in Internet Explorer and log in if prompted.

6. Navigate to the left-hand side of the page and select **Websites**.

7. Select the Azure website (for example, **psautoprimary**).

8. Under the **SCALE** section, set the **WEB HOSTING PLAN MODE** to **STANDARD**. Click on **SAVE** at the bottom of the page:

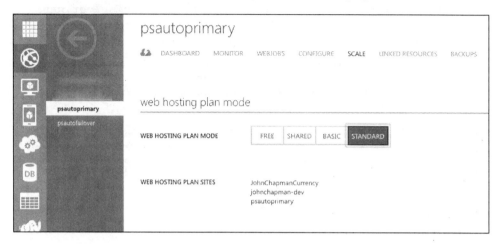

9. Repeat steps 6 to 8 for the second Azure website.

For more information about how to create and manage Microsoft Azure websites, refer to *Chapter 5, Deploying and Managing Azure Websites with PowerShell*.

Creating and managing Microsoft Azure Traffic Manager profiles

With the two Microsoft Azure websites created in the *Creating Microsoft Azure websites for load balancing* section, we can now create a new Microsoft Azure Traffic Manager profile to load-balance the two websites. We will use the following steps to load-balance the two websites with Traffic Manager:

1. Open Microsoft Azure PowerShell from the Start menu and connect it to an Azure subscription.

 We must first be connected to Azure in order to work with Microsoft Traffic Manager. If not connected to Azure, refer to the *Connecting to a Microsoft Azure subscription* section in *Chapter 1, Getting Started with Azure and PowerShell*.

2. Use the `New-AzureTrafficManagerProfile` cmdlet to create a new Traffic Manager profile. The `DomainName` parameter provided is where incoming requests will be directed and it must end with `.trafficmanager.net`. The `MonitorPort` parameter provided is the TCP/IP port to monitor the endpoints (for HTTP traffic, this is typically port 80):

```
PS C:\> New-AzureTrafficManagerProfile -Name "psautomation" -
DomainName "psautomation.trafficmanager.net" -
LoadBalancingMethod "Failover" -Ttl 30 -MonitorProtocol "Http"
-MonitorPort 80 -MonitorRelativePath "/"
```

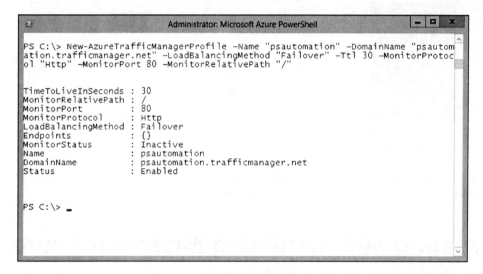

3. Use the `Get-AzureTrafficManagerProfile` cmdlet to assign the newly created Traffic Manager profile to a PowerShell variable:

```
PS C:\> $profile = Get-AzureTrafficManagerProfile -Name
"psautomation"
```

4. Use the `Add-AzureTrafficManagerEndpoint` and `Set-AzureTrafficManagerProfile` cmdlets to create a new endpoint for each Azure website and assign them to the Traffic Manager profile:

```
PS C:\> Add-AzureTrafficManagerEndpoint -TrafficManagerProfile
$profile -DomainName "psautoprimary.azurewebsites.net" -Status
"Enabled" -Type "AzureWebsite" | Set-
AzureTrafficManagerProfile
```

```
PS C:\> Add-AzureTrafficManagerEndpoint -TrafficManagerProfile
$profile -DomainName "psautofailover.azurewebsites.net" -
Status "Enabled" -Type "AzureWebsite" | Set-
AzureTrafficManagerProfile
```

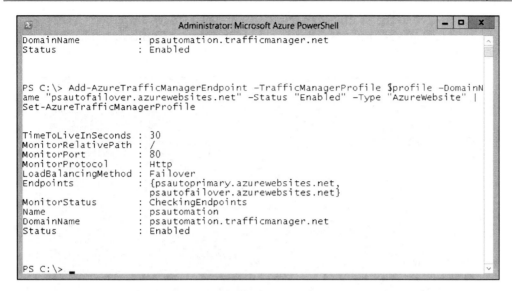

5. Use the `Get-AzureTrafficManagerProfile` cmdlet to ensure that the `MonitorStatus` is `Online` and the `Status` is `Enabled`:

PS C:\> Get-AzureTrafficManagerProfile –Name "PSAutomation"

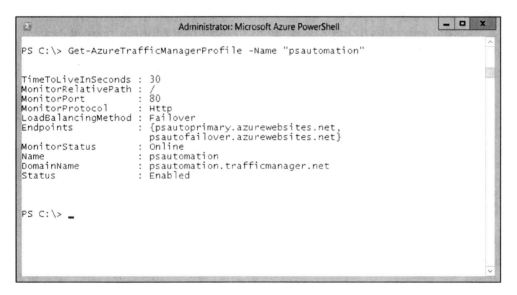

6. Navigate to the Traffic Manager domain name (for example, `http://psautomation.trafficmanager.net`) in Internet Explorer to observe the results:

7. Use the `Stop-AzureWebsite` cmdlet to stop the primary Azure website:

```
PS C:\> Stop-AzureWebsite -Name psautoprimary
```

8. Use the `Get-AzureTrafficManagerProfile` cmdlet to display the status of the endpoints (it might take up to 30 seconds for the endpoint status to update):

```
PS C:\> (Get-AzureTrafficManagerProfile -Name
"psautomation").Endpoints
```

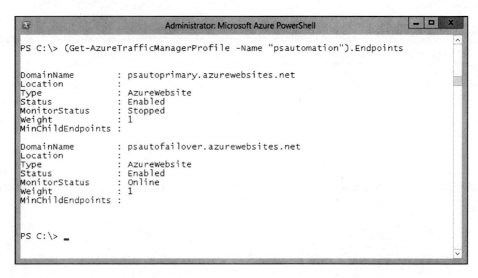

9. Use the `Get-AzureTrafficManagerProfile` cmdlet to assign the Traffic Manager profile to a PowerShell variable. We already did this in step 3. However, doing this again will retrieve an updated copy of the profile with the endpoints:

```
PS C:\> $profile = Get-AzureTrafficManagerProfile -Name
"psautomation"
```

10. Use the `Remove-AzureTrafficManagerEndpoint` and `Set-AzureTrafficManagerProfile` cmdlets to remove the primary endpoint from the Traffic Manager profile:

```
PS C:\> Remove-AzureTrafficManagerEndpoint -
TrafficManagerProfile $profile -DomainName
"psautoprimary.azurewebsites.net" | Set-
AzureTrafficManagerProfile
```

11. Use the `Remove-AzureTrafficManagerProfile` cmdlet to remove the Traffic Manager profile from the Microsoft Azure subscription:

```
PS C:\> Remove-AzureTrafficManagerProfile -Name "psautomation"
```

For more information about the cmdlets used in this section, use the `Get-Help` cmdlet in PowerShell, or refer to the following resources:

- The `Remove-AzureTrafficManagerProfile` cmdlet (https://msdn. microsoft.com/en-us/library/azure/dn690247.aspx)

- The `Remove-AzureTrafficManagerEndpoint` cmdlet (https://msdn. microsoft.com/en-us/library/azure/dn690251.aspx)

- The `Set-AzureTrafficManagerProfile` cmdlet (https://msdn. microsoft.com/en-us/library/azure/dn690254.aspx)

- The `Get-AzureTrafficManagerProfile` cmdlet (https://msdn. microsoft.com/en-us/library/azure/dn690255.aspx)

- The `Add-AzureTrafficManagerEndpoint` cmdlet (https://msdn. microsoft.com/en-us/library/azure/dn690257.aspx)

- The `New-AzureTrafficManagerProfile` cmdlet (https://msdn. microsoft.com/en-us/library/azure/dn690246.aspx)

Summary

In this chapter, we explored load-balancing Microsoft Azure services with Microsoft Azure Traffic Manager. We covered how to create, manage, and remove Traffic Manager profiles and endpoints. In the next chapter, we will explore how to manage Microsoft Azure cloud services with PowerShell.

8
Managing Azure Cloud Services with PowerShell

Microsoft Azure offers a variety of ways to host websites and web services. In *Chapter 5, Deploying and Managing Azure Websites with PowerShell*, we covered how to host websites using Microsoft Azure websites. Websites and services can also be hosted in Microsoft Azure virtual machines, which we covered in *Chapter 3, Managing Azure Virtual Machines with PowerShell*. Microsoft Azure also offers a third option: cloud services. Under the hood, Azure Cloud Services make use of Azure virtual machine instances to host websites and services. However, they are fully managed by Microsoft Azure. Microsoft Azure handles all routine maintenance, operating system updates, and attempts to recover from hardware failures.

Microsoft Azure Cloud Service roles consist of an application (such as a website) and a configuration file. These roles can either be a web role, which hosts a web application, or a worker role, which is used for asynchronous or long-running tasks. Each instance of a cloud service role correlates to an Azure virtual machine that runs the cloud service. Cloud services provide easy scaling of instances, depending on the workload of the cloud service.

Microsoft Azure Cloud Service instances provide additional flexibility that Azure websites do not provide. For instance, the start-up items on the instances can be configured. In addition, any MSI-based application can be installed on the instances. Lastly, cloud services provide staging and production environments seamlessly. This provides a highly flexible environment that does not require server maintenance on the part of the Azure customer.

Determining which type of hosting to use for a particular application depends greatly on the application itself. Consider the following scenarios:

- A company has a legacy web application that only runs on older versions of Windows, such as Windows Server 2003. In this case, an Azure virtual machine would provide the flexibility required to run the legacy application.

- A company has an e-commerce website that uses a web application and a SQL database. In this case, an Azure website that uses an Azure SQL database would provide the required functionality.

- A payroll company receives a large number of incoming payroll processing requests from its customers via a website. The payroll is processed asynchronously and provided back to the customer via the website when complete. In this case, an Azure Cloud Service worker role could be used to handle all the asynchronous processing and an Azure Cloud Service web role could be used to provide the interface to the customers.

Microsoft Azure virtual machines also take advantage of Azure Cloud Services. When a new Azure virtual machine is created, a cloud service is also created along with it to provide access to the virtual machine with the **Remote Desktop Protocol (RDP)**. In this chapter, we will deploy and manage a cloud service for a simple web role. In addition, we will use a cloud service to connect to an Azure virtual machine with RDP.

For more information about Microsoft Azure cloud services, refer to the following resources:

- Microsoft Azure Cloud Services (`http://azure.microsoft.com/en-us/services/cloud-services/`)

- What is a cloud service? (`http://azure.microsoft.com/en-us/documentation/articles/cloud-services-what-is/`)

- Comparison between Microsoft Azure websites, cloud services, and virtual machines (`http://azure.microsoft.com/en-us/documentation/articles/choose-web-site-cloud-service-vm/`)

Connecting to a Microsoft Azure virtual machine with a Microsoft Azure Cloud Service

In *Chapter 3, Managing Azure Virtual Machines with PowerShell*, we created a new Microsoft Azure virtual machine. In that example, the virtual machine was named `PSAuto2012R2`, and the cloud service was named `PSAutomation2012R2`. We will use the following steps to manage this cloud service and connect to the virtual machine with RDP:

1. Open Microsoft Azure PowerShell from the Start menu and connect it to an Azure subscription.

> We must first be connected to Azure in order to create and manage cloud services. If not connected to Azure, refer to the *Connecting to a Microsoft Azure subscription* section in *Chapter 1, Getting Started with Azure and PowerShell*. In addition, we should have an Azure virtual machine up-and-running. Refer to *Chapter 3, Managing Azure Virtual Machines with PowerShell*, for more detail on how to create a new virtual machine.

2. Use the `Get-AzureService` cmdlet (`PS C:\> Get-AzureService`) to retrieve the Azure cloud services in the current Azure subscription, as shown here:

```
                      Select Administrator: Microsoft Azure PowerShell         _ □ X
PS C:\> Get-AzureService
VERBOSE: 9:19:06 AM - Begin Operation: Get-AzureService
VERBOSE: 9:19:07 AM - Completed Operation: Get-AzureService


ServiceName           : PSAutomation2012R2
Url                   : https://management.core.windows.net/a1a2ba9b-f41a-460
                        0-81d7-c348e101594b/services/hostedservices/PSAutomat
                        ion2012R2
Label                 : PSAutomation2012R2
Description           : Implicitly created hosted service2015-01-28 16:12
Location              : West US
AffinityGroup         :
Status                : Created
ExtendedProperties    : {[ResourceGroup, PSAutomation2012R2],
                        [ResourceLocation, West US]}
DateModified          : 1/28/2015 9:12:49 AM
DateCreated           : 1/28/2015 9:12:15 AM
ReverseDnsFqdn        :
WebWorkerRoleSizes    : {A5, A6, A7, ExtraLarge, ExtraSmall, Large, Medium,
                        Small}
VirtualMachineRoleSizes : {A5, A6, A7, Basic_A0, Basic_A1, Basic_A2, Basic_A3,
                        Basic_A4, ExtraLarge, ExtraSmall, Large, Medium,
                        Small}
OperationDescription  : Get-AzureService
OperationId           : e539b793-8416-61e5-9663-c6e709cfaea7
OperationStatus       : Succeeded


PS C:\> _
```

3. Use the `Get-AzureRole` cmdlet (`PS C:\> Get-AzureRole -ServiceName PSAutomation2012R2 -InstanceDetails`) to retrieve the details of the Azure cloud service instances:

```
                                Administrator: Microsoft Azure PowerShell           _ □ x

PS C:\> Get-AzureRole -ServiceName PSAutomation2012R2 -InstanceDetails
VERBOSE: 9:27:47 AM - Begin Operation: Get Deployment
VERBOSE: 9:27:47 AM - Completed Operation: Get Deployment


InstanceEndpoints              : {PowerShell, RemoteDesktop}
InstanceErrorCode              :
InstanceFaultDomain            : 0
InstanceName                   : PSAuto2012R2
InstanceSize                   : Small
InstanceStateDetails           :
InstanceStatus                 : ReadyRole
InstanceUpgradeDomain          : 0
RoleName                       : PSAuto2012R2
DeploymentID                   : b5e2672065a143fd8244f480fdc3719b
IPAddress                      : 100.73.0.84
PublicIPAddress                :
PublicIPName                   :
PublicIPIdleTimeoutInMinutes   :
ServiceName                    : PSAutomation2012R2
OperationDescription           : Get-AzureRole
OperationId                    : 92ffdbf4-2dd7-69e7-b188-f39a9a152e75
OperationStatus                : Succeeded


PS C:\> _
```

4. Use the `Get-AzureRole` cmdlet to retrieve the cloud service endpoints for the virtual machine cloud service instance. By default, there is an endpoint for remote desktop and an endpoint for remote PowerShell. Make a note of the public TCP/IP port for the remote desktop endpoint:

```
PS C:\> $role = Get-AzureRole -ServiceName PSAutomation2012R2
-RoleName PSAuto2012R2 -InstanceDetails

PS C:\> $role.InstanceEndpoints
```

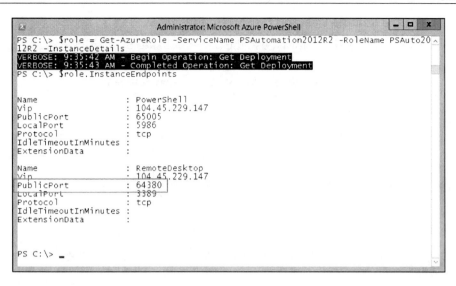

5. Open Remote Desktop Connection from the Start menu or using the `mstsc` command in the PowerShell window.

6. In the **Computer** field, enter the full URL for the Azure Cloud Service and the TCP/IP port number from step 4 as follows:

```
<Cloud Service Name>.cloudapp.net:<Port>
```

For instance:

```
psautomation2012r2.cloudapp.net:64380
```

7. Click on **Connect** and enter the credentials that were used when creating the virtual machine.

8. Close the **Remote Desktop Connection** window.

9. In the **PowerShell** window, use the `Get-AzureRemoteDesktopFile` cmdlet to save a RDP connection file on the local computer:

```
PS C:\> Get-AzureRemoteDesktopFile -ServiceName
PSAutomation2012R2 -Name PSAuto2012R2 -LocalPath
C:\RDP\PSAuto2012R2.rdp
```

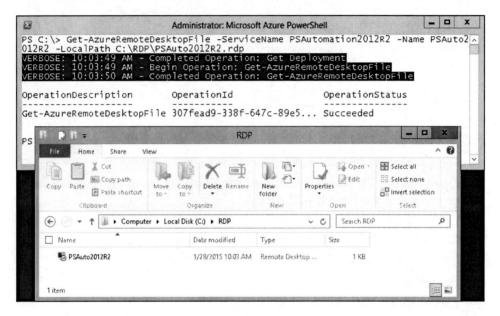

10. Double-click on the newly created RDP file in Windows Explorer to open Remote Desktop Connection and connect it to the virtual machine.

For more information about RDP and the cmdlets used in this section, refer to the following resources:

- The `Get-AzureService` cmdlet (https://msdn.microsoft.com/en-us/library/azure/dn495131.aspx)

- The `Get-AzureRole` cmdlet (https://msdn.microsoft.com/en-us/library/azure/dn495196.aspx)

- The `Get-AzureRemoteDesktopFile` cmdlet (https://msdn.microsoft.com/en-us/library/azure/dn495261.aspx)

- Remote Desktop Protocol (`https://msdn.microsoft.com/en-us/library/aa383015(v=vs.85).aspx`)

- Remote Desktop Protocol on Wikipedia (`http://en.wikipedia.org/wiki/Remote_Desktop_Protocol`)

Creating and managing Microsoft Azure Cloud Services

Deploying an application to a Microsoft Azure Cloud Service uses a cloud service package file that contains the application and a cloud service configuration file. Creating these files can be accomplished with Microsoft Visual Studio. However, this is outside the scope of this book. In order to publish a cloud service application in this section, a sample project has been included in the sample code of this book; this contains a cloud web role and a cloud worker role. Before you continue, ensure the files from the sample project are available on your computer.

We will use the following steps to create and manage an Azure Cloud Service with the sample application:

1. Open Microsoft Azure PowerShell from the Start menu and connect it to an Azure subscription.

> We must first be connected to Azure in order to create and manage cloud services. If not connected to Azure, refer to the *Connecting to a Microsoft Azure subscription* section in *Chapter 1, Getting Started with Azure and PowerShell.*

2. Use the `New-AzureService` cmdlet to create a new Azure Cloud Service:

```
PS C:\> New-AzureService -ServiceName "psautomation" -Location
"West US"
```

> In this example, we will use `West US` as the data center location for the new cloud service. To retrieve a full list of available locations to choose from, use the `Get-AzureLocation` cmdlet. For example, `Get-AzureLocation | Select-Object Name` will list only the names of the locations.

3. Use the `New-AzureDeployment` cmdlet and the sample application files to create a new deployment of the sample application cloud service:

    ```
    PS C:\> New-AzureDeployment -ServiceName psautomation -Package
    C:\Files\Azure\PSAutomationCloudService.cspkg -Configuration
    C:\Files\Azure\ServiceConfiguration.Cloud.cscfg -Slot
    Production
    ```

4. Use the `Get-AzureRole` cmdlet to display the instances created by the application deployment:

    ```
    PS C:\> Get-AzureRole -ServiceName psautomation -
    InstanceDetails
    ```

5. Use the `Remove-AzureDeployment` cmdlet to retract the deployment of the cloud service application:

```
PS C:\> Remove-AzureDeployment -ServiceName psautomation -Slot
Production
```

6. Use the `Get-AzureRole` cmdlet to verify that the deployment and the instances have been removed:

```
PS C:\> Get-AzureRole -ServiceName psautomation
```

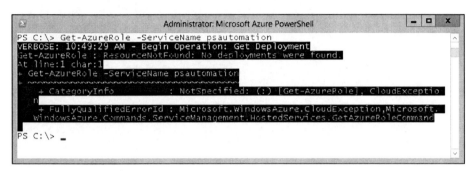

7. Use the `Remove-AzureService` cmdlet to remove the Azure Cloud Service from the Azure subscription:

```
PS C:\> Remove-AzureService -ServiceName psautomation
```

For more information about Azure Cloud Service applications and the cmdlets used in this section, refer to the following resources:

- Microsoft Azure Cloud Services documentation (http://azure.microsoft.com/en-us/documentation/services/cloud-services/)

- How to create and deploy a cloud service (http://azure.microsoft.com/en-us/documentation/articles/cloud-services-how-to-create-deploy/)

- Microsoft Azure downloads (http://azure.microsoft.com/en-us/downloads/)

- Get started with Azure Cloud Services and ASP.NET (http://azure.microsoft.com/en-us/documentation/articles/cloud-services-dotnet-get-started/)

- How to manage cloud services (http://azure.microsoft.com/en-us/documentation/articles/cloud-services-how-to-manage/)

- How to configure cloud services (http://azure.microsoft.com/en-us/documentation/articles/cloud-services-how-to-configure/)

Summary

Microsoft Azure Cloud Services provide an infrastructure to deploy large multitiered applications that include web and worker roles. In addition, cloud services provide endpoints to access Microsoft Azure virtual machines with remote PowerShell and RDP. In this chapter, we explored how to access a virtual machine with a cloud service. In addition, we created, deployed, and managed a new cloud service with a sample application.

In the next chapter, we will explore how to manage Microsoft Azure Active Directory.

9
Managing Azure Active Directory with PowerShell

By offering user and computer authentication and authorization, certificate management, group policy, federated services, and so on, Microsoft Active Directory is often the cornerstone of an organization's data center infrastructure. With Azure, the capabilities of Active Directory are extended to the cloud to provide features such as single sign-on with cloud services (including **Office 365** and **Salesforce.com**), multifactor authentication, and integration with existing on-premise deployments of Active Directory.

Azure utilizes Active Directory domains to manage authentication and authorization to Azure services. When a new Azure account is created, a default directory is automatically configured. The Microsoft account used for the Azure account is added to this directory as a Global Administrator.

Many organizations use scripting to manage their data center operations, and some organizations even require it. Active Directory is typically involved in these processes. In this chapter, we will explore how to automate some of the common tasks of Azure Active Directory management with PowerShell. However, Active Directory itself is a very large topic and one we will not cover in-depth in this chapter.

In this chapter, we will explore how to automate common tasks in Azure Active Directory management with PowerShell. We will cover the following topics:

- Connecting to Azure Active Directory
- Creating a new Azure Active Directory domain
- Configuring an Azure Active Directory domain
- Managing Azure Active Directory users and groups

- Using PowerShell to bulk-import users and groups to Azure Active Directory

A number of books and articles have been written about Active Directory. For more in-depth information about Active Directory, here are a few resources to get you started:

- The Active Directory Design Principles article by Packt Publishing (`https://www.packtpub.com/books/content/active-directory-design-principles-part-1`)
- The Active Directory Domain Services article by TechNet (`http://technet.microsoft.com/en-us/windowsserver/dd448614`)
- The book *Active Directory with PowerShell*, *Uma Yellapragada, Packt Publishing* (`https://www.packtpub.com/networking-and-servers/active-directory-powershell`)

Connecting to Azure Active Directory

The PowerShell tools for Azure Active Directory are separate from the tools used to manage other Azure services, which we covered in *Chapter 1, Getting Started with Azure and PowerShell*. Before you connect to Azure Active Directory, download and install the following tools:

- Microsoft Online Services Sign-In Assistant (`http://www.microsoft.com/en-us/download/details.aspx?id=41950`)
- Microsoft Azure Active Directory Module (`http://go.microsoft.com/fwlink/p/?linkid=236297`)

After installing these tools, reboot the computer to complete the installation.

If you use the Azure Active Directory module, you will encounter a known issue if you attempt to use the 32-bit version on a 64-bit computer. If you use the 32-bit version on a 64-bit computer and receive errors such as the term is not recognized, refer to `http://stackoverflow.com/questions/16018732/msonline-cant-be-imported-on-powershell-connect-msolservice-error`.

Creating an administrator account

Microsoft accounts and single sign-on accounts (for instance, using Active Directory Federation Services from an on-premise Active Directory domain) typically do not work to connect to Azure Active Directory in PowerShell. As a result, we will create a new Active Directory domain user in the Azure web portal that we can use to connect. To do this, follow these steps:

1. Log in to the Azure portal in a web browser at `https://manage.windowsazure.com`.

2. From the left-hand side navigation panel, select **ACTIVE DIRECTORY** and then select **Default Directory**, as shown in the following screenshot:

3. Select the **USERS** tab and then click on **ADD USER** at the bottom of the screen:

4. Enter the name in the **USER NAME** field and click on the next button:

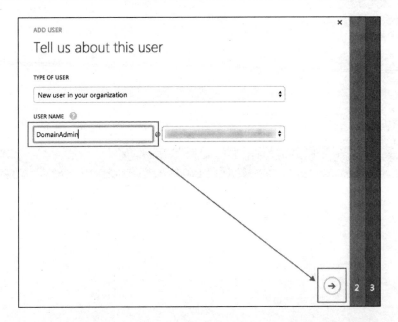

5. Select **Global Administrator** for **ROLE** and provide **FIRST NAME, LAST NAME, DISPLAY NAME**, and **ALTERNATE EMAIL ADDRESS** for the new user. Click on the next button:

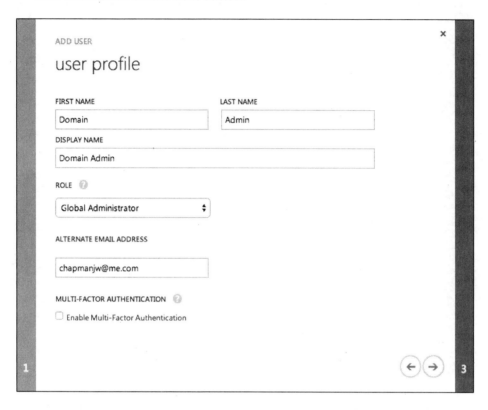

6. Click on **CREATE**.

7. Make a note of the full username and the temporary password for the new user:

8. To enable this user to create new Active Directory domains, rather than just manage the Default Directory, we will need to add this user as an Azure Administrator. From the left-hand side of the Azure management portal, select **SETTINGS, ADMINISTRATORS**, and then click on **ADD**, as shown in the following screenshot:

9. In the **EMAIL ADDRESS** field, enter the full username of the user we created (for example, DomainAdmin@azure.onmicrosoft.com), select **SUBSCRIPTION**, and click on the checkmark button to complete the process of adding the user:

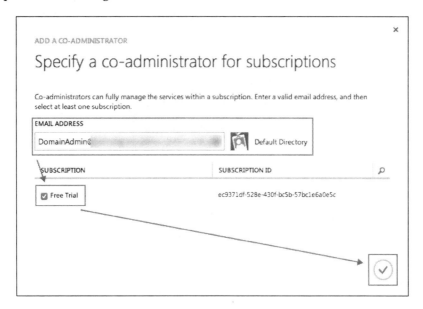

10. Before the newly created account can be used, we need to change the temporary password. First, log out from the Azure portal by selecting your account name in the top-right corner of the page and clicking on **SIGN OUT**.

11. Click on **SIGN IN** to return to the login page.

12. Use the username and temporary password of the newly created account to log in.

13. When prompted, provide a new password for the account.

With the new administrator account created and the password set, we can now connect to Azure Active Directory with PowerShell.

Connecting to Azure Active Directory

When we installed the Azure Active Directory module for PowerShell, the MSOnline module was registered with PowerShell. To make the cmdlets from the module available, we can either select the Windows Azure Active Directory Module for Windows PowerShell entry from the Start menu, or we can manually import the MSOnline module. To do this, follow these steps:

1. Open Windows Azure Active Directory Module for Windows PowerShell from the Start menu or add the module to an existing PowerShell session using the following command:

    ```
    PS C:\> Import-Module MSOnline
    ```

2. Use the Connect-MsolService cmdlet to connect to Azure Active Directory. You will be prompted to enter your credentials. Use the full username and password for the administrator account we created:

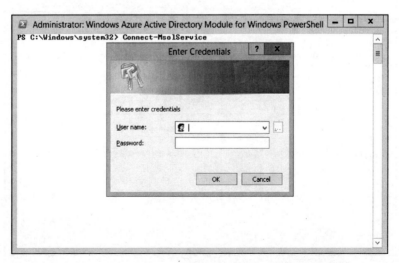

The PowerShell session is now connected to Azure Active Directory.

 In the event you receive an error message while attempting to connect to Azure Active Directory, Microsoft has some troubleshooting steps that will resolve most cases; refer to http://support.microsoft.com/kb/2494043.

For more information about Azure Active Directory and the cmdlet used in this section, refer to the following resources:

- What is Azure Active Directory? (http://azure.microsoft.com/en-us/documentation/articles/active-directory-whatis/)

- Manage Azure AD using Windows PowerShell (http://msdn.microsoft.com/en-us/library/azure/jj151815.aspx)

- The Connect-MsolService cmdlet (http://msdn.microsoft.com/en-us/library/azure/dn194123.aspx)

Creating a new Azure Active Directory domain

Each new Azure account includes a Default Directory with a default domain (for instance, azure.onmicrosoft.com) that contains the Microsoft account that created the Azure account. While the default domain might be sufficient for small organizations or organizations that do not use Azure Active Directory for their user authentication and authorization, larger organizations and organizations that rely heavily on Azure Active Directory will want to create a new Active Directory domain and customize it based on their needs.

Active Directory domains are assigned with fully qualified domain names. This provides a mechanism to find the domain within a network as well as to identify computers and so on within the domain. In a private network, Active Directory can work with a DNS server (domain name server) to ensure the domain name points to the Active Directory domain controllers (servers). However, with an Azure Active Directory domain, a public domain name from a registrar is required and the DNS settings for the domain are manually configured. In many organizations, a single group in the organization manages public domain names. DNS settings would have to be coordinated with this group. For other organizations or simple testing environments, a domain name will need to be purchased from GoDaddy.com, Name.com, or NetworkSolutions.com.

Before you continue, ensure that you are connected to Azure Active Directory in a PowerShell session, as outlined in the *Connecting to Azure Active Directory* section.

In this tutorial, we will use PowerShell to create a new Azure Active Directory domain in the default directory. However, we will not cover how to configure the DNS settings. Microsoft has provided instructions on how to configure the DNS settings at various registrars on MSDN (`http://msdn.microsoft.com/library/azure/jj151803.aspx#BKMK_cname`). To create a new Azure Active Directory domain in the default directory, follow these steps:

1. Use the `New-MsolDomain` cmdlet to create a new Active Directory domain and assign it to a PowerShell variable. The name provided should be in the form of a **fully qualified domain name (FQDN)**. It should match the domain name purchased from a registrar or should be provided by the group in the organization that manages public domain names:

    ```
    PS C:\> $domain = New-MsolDomain -Name PowerShell.local
    ```

2. Enter the variable and press *Enter*. The variable can be used to retrieve information about the new domain or to configure it:

    ```
    PS C:\> $domain
    ```

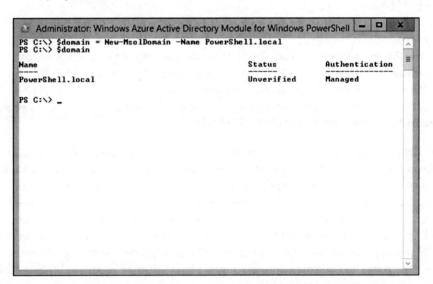

3. Use the `Get-MsolDomainVerificationDns` cmdlet to retrieve the label to be used when updating the DNS settings of the domain name:

    ```
    PS C:\> Get-MsolDomainVerificationDns -DomainName
    PowerShell.local
    ```

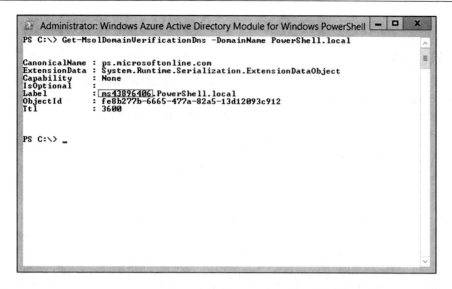

4. Use the label for the domain to add a TXT or MX record to the DNS settings for the domain name. In the sample used for the screenshots, the TXT record will be ms43896406, and the MX record will be ms43896406.msv1.invalid. Microsoft provides instructions to update the DNS records at many of the common domain name registrars on MSDN at http://msdn.microsoft.com/library/azure/jj151803.aspx#BKMK_cname.

 Once DNS records are updated, it can take up to 48 hours for them to propagate.

5. Once the DNS records for the domain are configured, use the Confirm-MsolDomain cmdlet to process the verification of the domain:

```
PS C:\> Confirm-MsolDomain -DomainName PowerShell.local
```

For more information about verifying domain names and the cmdlets used in this section, refer to the following resources:

- The New-MsolDomain cmdlet (http://msdn.microsoft.com/en-us/library/azure/dn194081.aspx)

- Verify a domain at any domain name registrar (http://msdn.microsoft.com/library/azure/jj151803.aspx)

- The Confirm-MsolDomain cmdlet (http://msdn.microsoft.com/en-us/library/azure/dn194117.aspx)

Configuring an Azure Active Directory domain

Once an Active Directory domain is created in Azure, there are a few options that can be configured for the domain. These options include converting to and from a federated domain, authentication settings, and password policy options.

 Before you continue, ensure that you are connected to Azure Active Directory in a PowerShell session, as outlined in the *Connecting to Azure Active Directory* section.

In this tutorial, we will configure the password policy for the domain that we created in the *Creating a new Azure Active Directory domain* section. The password policy includes two options: NotificationDays and ValidityPeriod. The NotificationDays option sets how many calendar days the password change notification should be sent before the password expires, and the ValidityPeriod option sets how many calendar days the passwords are valid for. To configure the password policy for the domain, follow these steps:

1. Use the Get-MsolPasswordPolicy cmdlet to view the current password policy settings. By default, nothing will be set for the NotificationDays and ValidityPeriod values:

   ```
   PS C:\> Get-MsolPasswordPolicy -DomainName PowerShell.local
   ```

2. Use the Set-MsolPasswordPolicy cmdlet to set the password policy settings:

   ```
   PS C:\> Set-MsolPasswordPolicy -DomainName PowerShell.local -
   NotificationDays 14 -ValidityPeriod 90
   ```

For more information about the cmdlets used in this section, use the Get-Help cmdlet in PowerShell, or refer to the following resources:

- The Get-MsolPasswordPolicy cmdlet (http://msdn.microsoft.com/en-us/library/azure/dn169219.aspx)

- The Set-MsolPasswordPolicy cmdlet (http://msdn.microsoft.com/en-us/library/azure/dn169224.aspx)

Managing Azure Active Directory users and groups

Active Directory can be used to manage a wide variety of objects, such as computers, users, contacts, and printers. Of all these objects, users and groups are the most commonly used. A user in Active Directory typically represents a person (or service accounts used by other applications) and provides a mechanism to store personal data about this person. A group in Active Directory can have users or other groups as members, but does not actually contain them and does not provide hierarchal organization to the domain; **organizational units** (OUs) provide hierarchal organization. Groups can have policies, authorization, and so on assigned to them that are inherited by the members in the group.

To illustrate how groups and users relate to each other, consider the following aspects:

- We have three groups: Services, Support, and Development
- We have two users: John and Jane
- The membership of each group is as follows:
    - Services: Support
    - Support: John
    - Development: Jane
- The Services group provides access to the Services file share, and the Development group provides access to the Development file share

In this example, Jane has access to the Development file share as she is a member of the Development group. In addition, John has access to the Services file share because he is a member of the Support group that is a member of the Services group.

For more information about how Active Directory domains are structured, refer to `http://en.wikipedia.org/wiki/Active_Directory`.

 Before you continue, ensure that you are connected to Azure Active Directory in a PowerShell session, as outlined in the *Connecting to Azure Active Directory* section.

For this tutorial, we will create users and groups (described in the preceding example). In addition, we will assign group membership. To do this, follow these steps:

1. Use the `New-MsolUser` cmdlet to create a user account for Jane and John and assign them to variables. The username must include the domain name, for example, `jane@powershell.local`, as shown here:

    ```
    PS C:\> $jane = New-MsolUser -UserPrincipalName
    "jane@powershell.local" -DisplayName "Jane" -Password
    "P@assword1234~"

    PS C:\> $john = New-MsolUser -UserPrincipalName
    "john@powershell.local" -DisplayName "John" -Password
    "P@assword1234~"
    ```

2. Use the `New-MsolGroup` cmdlet to create a group for Support, Services, and Development and assign them to variables:

    ```
    PS C:\> $services = New-MsolGroup -DisplayName "Services"

    PS C:\> $support = New-MsolGroup -DisplayName "Support"

    PS C:\> $development = New-MsolGroup -DisplayName
    "Development"
    ```

3. Use the `Add-MsolGroupMember` cmdlet to add Jane to the members of Development and John to the members of Support. In addition, assign Support to the members of Services:

    ```
    PS C:\> Add-MsolGroupMember -GroupObjectId
    $development.ObjectId -GroupMemberObjectId $jane.ObjectId

    PS C:\> Add-MsolGroupMember -GroupObjectId $support.ObjectId -
    GroupMemberObjectId $john.ObjectId

    PS C:\> Add-MsolGroupMember -GroupObjectId $services.ObjectId
    -GroupMemberObjectId $support.ObjectId -GroupMemberType Group
    ```

4. Use the `Get-MsolGroupMember` cmdlet to view the membership of each group:

    ```
    PS C:\> Get-MsolGroupMember -GroupObjectId $services.ObjectId
    ```

Users and groups in Azure Active Directory have a number of properties that can be set with PowerShell. Updating these properties can be done using the `Set-MsolUser` and `Set-MsolGroup` cmdlets (for example, `PS C:\> Set-MsolUser -ObjectId $jane.ObjectId -City "London"`).

For more information about Active Directory and the cmdlets used in this section, refer to the following resources:

*   Active Directory (`http://en.wikipedia.org/wiki/Active_Directory`)
*   The `New-MsolUser` cmdlet (`http://msdn.microsoft.com/en-us/library/azure/dn194096.aspx`)

- The `New-MsolGroup` cmdlet (http://msdn.microsoft.com/en-us/library/azure/dn194083.aspx)

- The `Set-MsolUser` cmdlet (http://msdn.microsoft.com/en-us/library/azure/dn194136.aspx)

- The `Set-MsolGroup` cmdlet (http://msdn.microsoft.com/en-us/library/azure/dn194086.aspx)

- The `Add-MsolGroupMember` cmdlet (http://msdn.microsoft.com/en-us/library/azure/dn194129.aspx)

- The `Get-MsolGroupMember` cmdlet (http://msdn.microsoft.com/en-us/library/azure/dn194085.aspx)

Using PowerShell to bulk import users and groups into Azure Active Directory

While running one-off commands in PowerShell can be useful, managing Azure Active Directory with PowerShell really comes into its own when scripting large amounts of tedious tasks. With PowerShell, we can complete a process in a few minutes that might take hours or days for a human to complete manually.

Imagine a medium-sized company with about 1,000 users. The company's human resources system has details (such as names and contact information exported to a spreadsheet in CSV format). The company implements Azure services as part of the company infrastructure and needs to create a user account in Azure Active Directory for each user. Someone could take days to complete it manually in the web interface but, with PowerShell, this can be done in just a few minutes.

 Before you continue, ensure that you are connected to Azure Active Directory in a PowerShell session, as outlined in the *Connecting to Azure Active Directory* section.

In this tutorial, we will create a `.csv` file with some user details, and we will use this data to create users in Azure Active Directory with PowerShell. To do this, follow these steps:

1. Create a `.csv` file with data that looks like the following code snippet:

```
"Username","Password","DisplayName","City"
"rose@powershell.local","P@ssword1234~","Rose","London"
"jose@powershell.local","P@ssword1234~","Jose","London"
"pierre@powershell.local","P@ssword1234~","Pierre","London"
"diego@powershell.local","P@ssword1234~","Diego","London"
"sherlock@powershell.local","P@ssword1234~","Sherlock","London"
```

You can create the `.csv` file with any plain text editor (such as Notepad) or spreadsheet software (such as Microsoft Excel).

2. Use the `Import-Csv` cmdlet to import the user data from the `.csv` file to a PowerShell object:

    ```
    PS C:\> $users = Import-Csv C:\Files\Users.csv
    ```

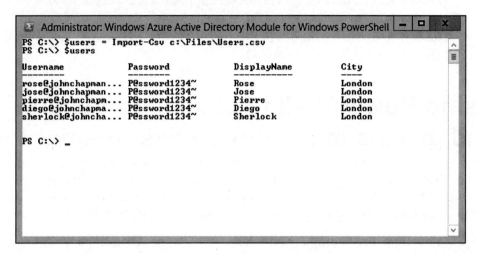

3. Use the `ForEach-Object` and `New-MsolUser` cmdlets to enumerate each user in the imported data and create the user account:

    ```
    PS C:\> $users | ForEach-Object { New-MsolUser -
    UserPrincipalName $_.Username -Password $_.Password -
    DisplayName $_.DisplayName -City $_.City }
    ```

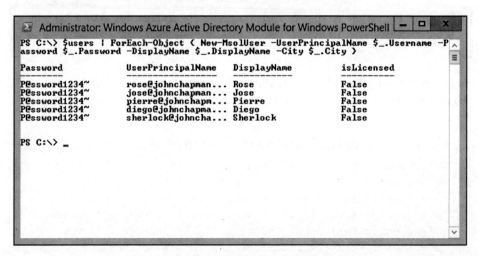

For more information about the cmdlets used in this section, use the `Get-Help` cmdlet in PowerShell, or refer to the following resources:

- The `Import-Csv` cmdlet (`http://technet.microsoft.com/en-us/library/hh849891.aspx`)

- The `ForEach-Object` cmdlet (`http://technet.microsoft.com/en-us/library/hh849731.aspx`)

- The `New-MsolUser` cmdlet (`http://msdn.microsoft.com/en-us/library/azure/dn194096.aspx`)

Summary

Azure Active Directory offers a myriad of features and services for Azure customers. In this chapter, we covered the basics of how to manage Azure Active Directory from PowerShell and showcased an example where PowerShell automation can save administrators time and effort. Using these techniques and ideas, many mundane and repetitive tasks can be automated to allow administrators to focus on more important tasks.

In the next chapter, we will explore how to automate Microsoft Azure tasks in PowerShell using runbooks and automation cmdlets.

10
Automating Azure with PowerShell

Throughout this book, we have covered individual management tasks from uploading files to blob storage to creating users in Active Directory. Each of the individual tasks we covered gave us an opportunity to simplify and streamline managing Azure services from PowerShell. Many organizations have complex tasks that utilize a number of separate individual commands to complete. These tasks can be long, tedious, and error-prone. In addition, many of these tasks are scheduled to run automatically on a repeating schedule.

For example, a company might need to back up an Azure website and Azure SQL database on an hourly schedule. Completing this task manually every hour would be difficult to accomplish. The company can use a scheduled task in Windows (either on a local computer or in an Azure virtual machine) to perform the tasks. However, this takes up resources and requires a computer to be running constantly.

To simplify the repetitive and complex tasks that administrators perform with Azure, Microsoft Azure Automation provides a framework to create and schedule workflows. These workflows, also known as **runbooks**, are PowerShell scripts that define a series of tasks to perform when run. In this chapter, we will explore Microsoft Azure Automation by creating and managing runbooks.

Creating a Microsoft Azure Automation account

Runbooks in Microsoft Azure run within the context of an Azure Automation account. Before we create and manage runbooks, we will first create a new Azure Automation account and a set of credentials to access Azure Automation with. Storing credentials in Azure Automation allows workflows to connect to Azure as the account provided.

We will use the following steps to create a new account and credentials:

1. Log in to the Microsoft Azure management portal in Internet Explorer at `https://manage.windowsazure.com`.

2. From the left-hand side navigation menu, click on **AUTOMATION**.

3. Select **CREATE AN AUTOMATION ACCOUNT**, as shown in the following screenshot:

4. Enter a name for the new account and select a region:

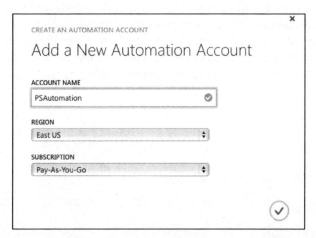

5. Next click on the checkmark to finish the process.

6. Now select the newly created Azure Automation account.

7. Click on the **ASSETS** tab, as shown here:

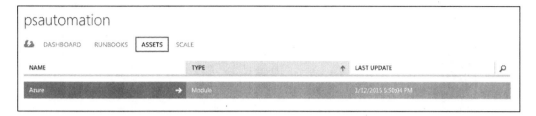

8. Select **ADD SETTING** at the bottom of the page.

9. Next select **ADD CREDENTIAL** to add the type of setting.

10. Select **Windows PowerShell Credential** as **CREDENTIAL TYPE** and enter PSAutomation as the name of the credential:

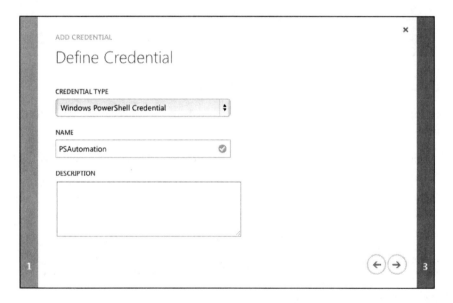

11. Provide a username and password for the credentials. We will use the username and password of the Microsoft account that we used to manage Microsoft Azure:

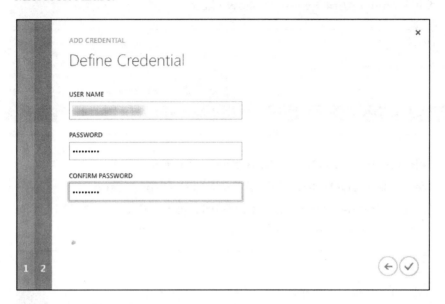

12. Finally, click on the checkmark to finish the process.

For more information about Microsoft Azure Automation accounts, refer to the following resources:

- Microsoft Azure Automation (`https://msdn.microsoft.com/en-us/library/azure/dn643629.aspx`)

- Microsoft Azure Automation accounts (`https://msdn.microsoft.com/en-us/library/azure/dn794195.aspx`)

Creating and managing runbooks in Microsoft Azure

With the Microsoft Azure Automation account and credentials created in the *Creating a Microsoft Azure Automation account* section, we can now create and manage runbooks. We will use the following steps to create and manage runbooks:

1. Open Microsoft Azure PowerShell from the Start menu and connect it to an Azure subscription.

 We must first be connected to Azure in order to create and manage runbooks. If not connected to Azure, refer to the *Connecting to a Microsoft Azure subscription* section in *Chapter 1, Getting Started with Azure and PowerShell.*

2. Use the New-AzureAutomationRunbook cmdlet to create a new runbook:

   ```
   PS C:\> New-AzureAutomationRunbook –Name "PSAutomationStarter"
   –AutomationAccountName psautomation
   ```

3. Open Notepad or any plain text editor of your choice.

4. Define the runbook workflow with the following code:

   ```
   workflow PSAutomationStarter
   {
       # Retrieve credentials from the Automation account
       $creds = Get-AutomationPSCredential -Name 'PSAutomation'

       # Connect to the Azure account
       Add-AzureAccount -Credential $creds

       # Select Azure subscription
       Select-AzureSubscription -SubscriptionName 'Pay-As-You-
   Go'

       # Get the Azure virtual machines in the Azure
   subscription
       Get-AzureVM
   }
   ```

 In this workflow, we are retrieving the credentials we stored in the Automation account, connecting to Azure, selecting an Azure subscription, and getting a list of the Azure virtual machines in the Azure subscription. To get the name of your Azure subscription, use the Get-AzureSubscription cmdlet.

5. Save the runbook workflow as a .ps1 file, for example, C:\Files\Azure\PSAutomationStarter.ps1.

6. Use the `Set-AzureAutomationRunbookDefinition` cmdlet to set the runbook workflow for the runbook we created in step 2:

   ```
   PS C:\> Set-AzureAutomationRunbookDefinition –Name
   |"PSAutomationStarter" –Path
   C:\Files\Azure\PSAutomationStarter.ps1 –AutomationAccountName
   psautomation -Overwrite
   ```

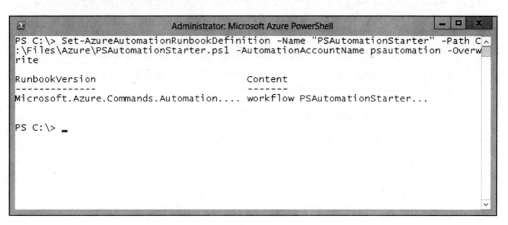

7. Use the `Publish-AzureAutomationRunbook` cmdlet to publish the runbook workflow and make it available for use:

   ```
   PS C:\> Publish-AzureAutomationRunbook –Name
   PSAutomationStarter –AutomationAccountName psautomation
   ```

8. Use the `Start-AzureAutomationRunbook` cmdlet to run the runbook workflow:

   ```
   PS C:\> Start-AzureAutomationRunbook –Name PSAutomationStarter
   –AutomationAccountName psautomation
   ```

9. Use the `Get-AzureAutomationJob` cmdlet to check the status of the runbook workflow:

   ```
   PS C:\> Get-AzureAutomationJob –RunbookName
   PSAutomationStarter –AutomationAccountName psautomation
   ```

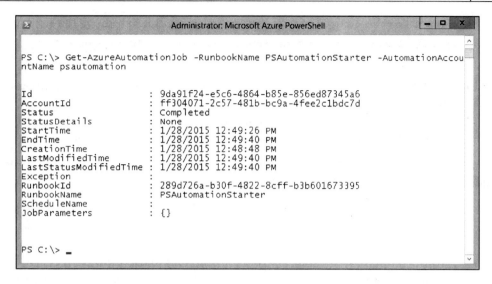

```
Administrator: Microsoft Azure PowerShell                          — □ X

PS C:\> Get-AzureAutomationJob -RunbookName PSAutomationStarter -AutomationAccou
ntName psautomation

Id                     : 9da91f24-e5c6-4864-b85e-856ed87345a6
AccountId              : ff304071-2c57-481b-bc9a-4fee2c1bdc7d
Status                 : Completed
StatusDetails          : None
StartTime              : 1/28/2015 12:49:26 PM
EndTime                : 1/28/2015 12:49:40 PM
CreationTime           : 1/28/2015 12:48:48 PM
LastModifiedTime       : 1/28/2015 12:49:40 PM
LastStatusModifiedTime : 1/28/2015 12:49:40 PM
Exception              :
RunbookId              : 289d726a-b30f-4822-8cff-b3b601673395
RunbookName            : PSAutomationStarter
ScheduleName           :
JobParameters          : {}


PS C:\> _
```

10. If the status returns `Completed`, use the `Get-AzureAutomationJobOutput` cmdlet to retrieve the output from the runbook workflow, using the ID returned from the previous step:

    ```
    PS C:\> Get-AzureAutomationJobOutput -Id 9da91f24-e5c6-4864-
    b85e-856ed87345a6 -Stream Any -AutomationAccountName
    psautomation
    ```

11. Use the `New-AzureAutomationSchedule` cmdlets to create a new schedule:

    ```
    PS C:\> New-AzureAutomationSchedule -Name "DailyReport" -
    StartTime (Get-Date).AddDays(1) -ExpiryTime (Get-
    Date).AddDays(31) -Description "Daily report of VMs" -
    AutomationAccountName psautomation
    ```

12. Use the `Register-AzureAutomationScheduledRunbook` cmdlet to associate the runbook workflow with the newly created schedule:

    ```
    PS C:\> Register-AzureAutomationScheduledRunbook -ScheduleName
    "DailyReport" -Name "PSAutomationStarter" -
    AutomationAccountName psautomation
    ```

13. Use the `Unregister-AzureAutomationScheduledRunbook` cmdlet to remove the association with the schedule:

    ```
    PS C:\> Unregister-AzureAutomationScheduledRunbook -
    ScheduleName "DailyReport" -Name "PSAutomationStarter" -
    AutomationAccountName psautomation
    ```

14. Use the `Remove-AzureAutomationSchedule` cmdlet to remove the schedule:

    ```
    PS C:\> Remove-AzureAutomationSchedule -Name "DailyReport" -
    AutomationAccountName psautomation
    ```

15. Use the `Remove-AzureAutomationRunbook` cmdlet to remove the runbook workflow:

    ```
    PC C:\> Remove-AzureAutomationRunbook -Name
    PSAutomationStarter -AutomationAccountName psautomation
    ```

For more information about Microsoft Azure Automation, runbooks, and the cmdlets used in this section, refer to the following resources:

- Microsoft Azure Automation in Depth: Runbook Authoring (http://azure.microsoft.com/blog/2014/07/03/azure-automation-in-depth-runbook-authoring/)

- Azure Automation: Runbook Input, Output, and Nested Runbooks (http://azure.microsoft.com/blog/2014/08/12/azure-automation-runbook-input-output-and-nested-runbooks/)

- The `New-Azure AutomationRunbook` cmdlet (https://msdn.microsoft.com/en-us/library/dn690272.aspx)

- The `Set-AzureAutomationRunbookDefinition` cmdlet (https://msdn.microsoft.com/en-us/library/dn690267.aspx)

- The `Publish-AzureAutomationRunbook` cmdlet (https://msdn.microsoft.com/en-us/library/dn690266.aspx)

- The `Start-AzureAutomationRunbook` cmdlet (https://msdn.microsoft.com/en-us/library/dn690259.aspx)

- The `Get-AzureAutomationJob` cmdlet (https://msdn.microsoft.com/en-us/library/dn690263.aspx)

- The `Get-AzureAutomationJobOutput` cmdlet (https://msdn.microsoft.com/en-us/library/dn690268.aspx)

- The `New-AzureAutomationSchedule` cmdlet (https://msdn.microsoft.com/en-us/library/dn690271.aspx)

- The `Register-AzureAutomationScheduledRunbook` cmdlet (https://msdn.microsoft.com/en-us/library/dn690265.aspx)

- The `Unregister-AzureAutomationScheduledRunbook` cmdlet (https://msdn.microsoft.com/en-us/library/dn690273.aspx)

- The `Remove-AzureAutomationSchedule` cmdlet (https://msdn.microsoft.com/en-us/library/dn690279.aspx)

- The `Remove-AzureAutomationRunbook` cmdlet (https://msdn.microsoft.com/en-us/library/dn690264.aspx)

Summary

Microsoft Azure Automation provides a framework to streamline, automate, and simplify complex and repetitive Azure management tasks. In this chapter, we started out with creating a new Azure Automation account. We then created and managed a simple Azure Automation runbook workflow. Using these techniques, nearly any Microsoft Azure management task can be automated and scheduled.

Throughout this book, we explored how to use PowerShell to manage several Microsoft Azure services. This book was by no means exhaustive. There are many Azure services that we did not cover, such as RemoteApp, Machine Learning, Media Services, Service Bus, Visual Studio Online, and Operational Insights. Microsoft is continually improving its existing services and features and simultaneously adding new ones. We encourage you to explore and discover what Microsoft Azure has to offer. Visit http://azure.microsoft.com/en-us/ to see all of the current Microsoft Azure offerings. Keep yourself up-to-date with the latest Microsoft Azure announcements on the Microsoft Azure blog (http://azure.microsoft.com/blog/). Also, check out the new and upcoming preview features of Microsoft Azure at http://azure.microsoft.com/en-us/services/preview/.

We used Microsoft Azure PowerShell to accomplish most of the tasks throughout this book. Microsoft Azure PowerShell is an open source project with new and updated cmdlets added every month to make managing Azure services with PowerShell more compelling, streamlined, and reproducible. The agility of this toolset is made possible with the contributions of over one hundred contributors to the project from around the globe. If you would like to contribute ideas, code, bug fixes, and so on to the Microsoft Azure PowerShell project, refer to the project on GitHub at https://github.com/Azure/azure-powershell.

Lastly, it's our sincere hope that the information in this book proves to be a valuable foundation for you in managing Microsoft Azure with PowerShell. As you explore the additional capabilities of Microsoft Azure and Microsoft Azure PowerShell, it's more than likely that you will have questions. The Microsoft Azure forums (https://social.msdn.microsoft.com/forums/azure/en-US/home) and Stack Overflow (http://stackoverflow.com/questions/tagged/azure) are excellent resources to discuss Microsoft Azure and Azure PowerShell with other IT and development professionals from around the world.

Index

O

Office 365 99
organizational units (OUs) 111

P

permission levels, Azure Blog storage
  blob 25
  container 25
  off 25
point-to-site VPN 72
PowerShell Community Extensions
  URL 35
PowerShell ISE 4
Publish-AzureAutomationRunbook cmdlet
  URL 124
publish settings file
  used, for connecting to Azure 11-14

R

Register-AzureAutomationScheduled
    Runbook cmdlet
  URL 124
Remote Desktop Protocol (RDP)
  URL 95
Remove-AzureAutomationRunbook cmdlet
  URL 124
Remove-AzureDataDisk cmdlet
  URL 48
Remove-AzureStorageAccount cmdlet
  URL 19
Remove-AzureTrafficManagerEndpoint
    cmdlet
  URL 87
Remove-AzureTrafficManagerProfile cmdlet
  URL 87
Remove-AzureVM cmdlet
  URL 50
Remove-AzureVNetConfig cmdlet
  URL 78
Remove-AzureWebsite cmdlet
  URL 69
Restart-AzureVM cmdlet
  URL 45

runbooks
  about 117
  creating, in Azure 120-124
  managing, in Azure 120-124
  resources 124

S

Salesforce.com 99
Select-Object cmdlet
  URL 42
Server Message Block (SMB) protocol 20
Set-AzureAutomationRunbookDefinition
    cmdlet
  URL 124
Set-AzureStorageBlobContent cmdlet
  URL 26
Set-AzureStorageFileContent cmdlet
  URL 24
Set-AzureTrafficManagerProfile cmdlet
  URL 87
Set-AzureVNetConfig cmdlet
  URL 76
Set-AzureWebsite cmdlet
  URL 66
Set-Content cmdlet
  URL 24
Set-MsolGroup cmdlet
  URL 113
Set-MsolPasswordPolicy cmdlet
  URL 110
Set-MsolUser cmdlet
  URL 113
Show-AzureWebsite cmdlet
  URL 66
site-to-site VPN 71
software prerequisites, Microsoft Azure
    connection
  Microsoft Azure PowerShell 7
  Windows PowerShell 3.0 6, 7
Start-AzureAutomationRunbook cmdlet
  URL 124
Start-AzureSqlDatabaseExport cmdlet
  URL 62

Thank you for buying

Automating Microsoft Azure with PowerShell

About Packt Publishing

Packt, pronounced 'packed', published its first book, *Mastering phpMyAdmin for Effective MySQL Management*, in April 2004, and subsequently continued to specialize in publishing highly focused books on specific technologies and solutions.

Our books and publications share the experiences of your fellow IT professionals in adapting and customizing today's systems, applications, and frameworks. Our solution-based books give you the knowledge and power to customize the software and technologies you're using to get the job done. Packt books are more specific and less general than the IT books you have seen in the past. Our unique business model allows us to bring you more focused information, giving you more of what you need to know, and less of what you don't.

Packt is a modern yet unique publishing company that focuses on producing quality, cutting-edge books for communities of developers, administrators, and newbies alike. For more information, please visit our website at www.packtpub.com.

About Packt Enterprise

In 2010, Packt launched two new brands, Packt Enterprise and Packt Open Source, in order to continue its focus on specialization. This book is part of the Packt Enterprise brand, home to books published on enterprise software – software created by major vendors, including (but not limited to) IBM, Microsoft, and Oracle, often for use in other corporations. Its titles will offer information relevant to a range of users of this software, including administrators, developers, architects, and end users.

Writing for Packt

We welcome all inquiries from people who are interested in authoring. Book proposals should be sent to author@packtpub.com. If your book idea is still at an early stage and you would like to discuss it first before writing a formal book proposal, then please contact us; one of our commissioning editors will get in touch with you.

We're not just looking for published authors; if you have strong technical skills but no writing experience, our experienced editors can help you develop a writing career, or simply get some additional reward for your expertise.

PowerShell 3.0 Advanced
Administration Handbook

ISBN: 978-1-84968-642-6   Paperback: 370 pages

A fast-paced PowerShell guide with real-world scenarios and detailed solutions

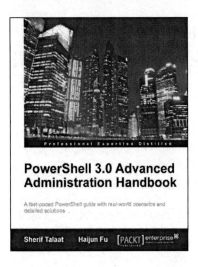

1. Discover and understand the concept of Windows PowerShell 3.0.

2. Learn the advanced topics and techniques for a professional PowerShell scripting.

3. Explore the secret of building custom PowerShell snap-ins and modules.

4. Take advantage of PowerShell integration capabilities with other technologies for better administration skills.

Microsoft Windows Azure
Development Cookbook

ISBN: 978-1-84968-222-0   Paperback: 392 pages

Over 80 advanced recipes for developing scalable services with the Windows Azure platform

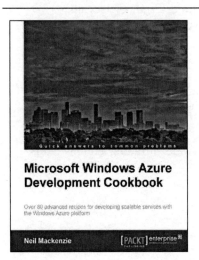

1. Packed with practical, hands-on recipes for building advanced, scalable cloud-based services on the Windows Azure platform explained in detail to maximize your learning.

2. Extensive code samples showing how to use advanced features of Windows Azure blobs, tables, and queues.

3. Understand remote management of Azure services using the Windows Azure Service Management REST API.

Please check **www.PacktPub.com** for information on our titles

Windows Azure Programming Patterns for Start-ups

ISBN: 978-1-84968-560-3   Paperback: 292 pages

A step-by-step guide to create easy solutions to build your business using Windows Azure services

1. Explore the different features of Windows Azure and its unique concepts.

2. Get to know the Windows Azure platform by code snippets and samples by a single start-up scenario throughout the whole book.

3. A clean example scenario demonstrates the different Windows Azure features.

Instant Windows PowerShell

ISBN: 978-1-84968-874-1   Paperback: 54 pages

Manage and automate your Windows Server Environment efficiently using PowerShell

1. Learn something new in an Instant! A short, fast, focused guide delivering immediate results.

2. Learn to use PowerShell web access to secure Windows management anywhere, any time, on any device.

3. Understand to secure and sign the scripts you write using the script signing feature in PowerShell.

Please check **www.PacktPub.com** for information on our titles

Lightning Source UK Ltd.
Milton Keynes UK
UKOW03f0800210415

250014UK00010B/356/P